BECOMING *One*

BECOMING *One*

Quiet Times
for Every Couple

GREG LAURIE

New York • Boston • Nashville

Unless otherwise noted, Scripture quotations are taken from the HOLY BIBLE: NEW INTER-NATIONAL VERSION®. NIV®. Copyright © 1973, 1978, 1984 by International Bible Society. Used by permission of Zondervan Publishing House. All rights reserved.

Scriptures noted NKJV are taken from the NEW KING JAMES VERSION. Copyright © 1979, 1980, 1982, Thomas Nelson, Inc., Publishers. Used by permission. All rights reserved.

Scriptures noted KJV are taken from the King James version of the Bible.

Scriptures noted NLT are from the *Holy Bible*, New Living Translation, copyright © 1996. Used by permission of Tyndale House Publishers, Inc., Wheaton, Illinois 60189. All rights reserved.

Portions of this book were previously published under the title *Marriage Connections* (Wheaton, IL: Tyndale House Publishers, 2003).

FaithWords
Hachette Book Group USA
237 Park Avenue
New York, NY 10017

Visit our Web site at www.faithwords.com

Printed in the United States of America
First Edition: January 2008

10 9 8 7 6 5 4 3 2 1

FaithWords is a division of Hachette Book Group USA, Inc.
The FaithWords name and logo is a trademark of Hachette Book Group USA, Inc.
Text design by Meryl Sussman Levavi

Library of Congress Cataloging-in-Publication Data
Laurie, Greg.
  Becoming one : quiet times for every couple / Greg Laurie.—1st ed.
    p. cm.
  ISBN-13: 978-0-446-50014-2
  ISBN-10: 0-446-50014-3
  1. Spouses—Prayers and devotions. 2. Marriage—Religious aspects—Christianiy—Meditations.
I. Title.
  BV4596.M3L385 2007
  242'.644—dc22   2007006515

BECOMING *One*

Quiet Times
for Every Couple

GREG LAURIE

New York • Boston • Nashville

Unless otherwise noted, Scripture quotations are taken from the HOLY BIBLE: NEW INTERNATIONAL VERSION®. NIV®. Copyright © 1973, 1978, 1984 by International Bible Society. Used by permission of Zondervan Publishing House. All rights reserved.

Scriptures noted NKJV are taken from the NEW KING JAMES VERSION. Copyright © 1979, 1980, 1982, Thomas Nelson, Inc., Publishers. Used by permission. All rights reserved.

Scriptures noted KJV are taken from the King James version of the Bible.

Scriptures noted NLT are from the *Holy Bible*, New Living Translation, copyright © 1996. Used by permission of Tyndale House Publishers, Inc., Wheaton, Illinois 60189. All rights reserved.

Portions of this book were previously published under the title *Marriage Connections* (Wheaton, IL: Tyndale House Publishers, 2003).

FaithWords
Hachette Book Group USA
237 Park Avenue
New York, NY 10017

Visit our Web site at www.faithwords.com

Printed in the United States of America
First Edition: January 2008

10 9 8 7 6 5 4 3 2 1

FaithWords is a division of Hachette Book Group USA, Inc.
The FaithWords name and logo is a trademark of Hachette Book Group USA, Inc.
Text design by Meryl Sussman Levavi

Library of Congress Cataloging-in-Publication Data
Laurie, Greg.
    Becoming one : quiet times for every couple / Greg Laurie.—1st ed.
        p. cm.
    ISBN-13: 978-0-446-50014-2
    ISBN-10: 0-446-50014-3
    1. Spouses—Prayers and devotions. 2. Marriage—Religious aspects—Christianiy—Meditations.
I. Title.
    BV4596.M3L385 2007
    242'.644—dc22   2007006515

To the bride of my youth,

best friend, and counselor—Catherine

To the bride of my youth,

best friend, and counselor—Catherine

CONTENTS

Week 8: A Christ-Centered Marriage

Week 9: Kindness and Respect

Week 10: Contented and Fulfilled

AUTHOR'S NOTE

*A*nother book on marriage?

There are already hundreds, even thousands, out there! Why another?

That is a valid question.

Let me say first that this is my first full-length devotional book on marriage.

And I have been married one time to one woman for thirty-three years now. People seem shocked by two things when I tell them that. First of all, that seems like a long time to be married in this age of quick divorces. But people are even more surprised that my wife, who looks thirty-three, has been married thirty-three years!

We have a happy, but not perfect, marriage. We have what some people call "irreconcilable differences." She is very neat, I am generally messy. She is often late, I am usually a bit early. She is more quiet, I am more outgoing. But rather than let this drive us apart, we say, *"Vive la difference!"* Cathe Laurie, whom you will be introduced to in the pages of this book, is my closest friend as well as lover and, of course, spouse.

As a pastor, I have also counseled and married many couples over the years. I must say it's been heartbreaking to see some of those couples not make it because they chose to disregard what God's Word says. But what sheer joy it has been to see so many that I have had the privilege of marrying go now for decades and welcome children and grandchildren.

There is another reason I feel qualified and, more then that, called to write a book on marriage.

I am a child from a divorced home.

That's almost an understatement in my case.

My mom was not married and divorced just once, or even twice, but seven times. I have seen divorce up close and personal, and it is painful and its repercussions are long-lasting. That is one of the reasons I was so determined to find and be the right person for and prayerfully have a marriage that would last a lifetime.

I try to be as candid as possible in this book about my own challenges and struggles as a married man, but my main objective is to point you to the Word of God. The Bible has so much to say about how to have a blessed and strong marriage as you learn more about what it means to become one.

Each of these devotionals closes with a section calling you to *Ponder, Probe,* and finally to *Pray.* Included are many quotes from a variety of sources intended to stimulate your thinking. My using these quotes is not an endorsement of all the writers say or think—merely an appreciation of their words on marriage. Let their words inform your own thinking as you invest in your marriage.

My prayer is that, when you are finished reading this book, your marriage will be stronger than it has ever been. May the Lord bless you and keep you and cause His face to shine upon you and give you peace as you seek to be the husband or wife He has called you to be.

LIKE NEW

This week, think about why you are doing this devotional. What does it mean to "become one"? How can your marriage become "like new"? This is the time to focus and settle into a new season: a twelve-week season of rejuvenating your marriage and revitalizing your walk with the Lord.

PLUG INTO THE SOURCE

Be filled with the Spirit.
EPHESIANS 5:18

Imagine going shopping and bringing home a new, state-of-the-art laptop computer. You are so excited! It's got built-in wi-fi so you can surf the web and play online games wherever you are. It has a CD and DVD drive so you can watch movies or listen to your favorite music. It has a beautiful wide screen and holds about a million gigs of data. You power it up and immediately start e-mailing everyone you know. There's no stopping you!

Until . . . suddenly your beloved computer dies. The screen goes dark, all those little buzzing noises stop, and nothing will get that laptop to come alive again. So you return it to the store.

"What's wrong with it?" the salesperson asks.

"It's dead!" you tell him. "It doesn't work. It's a lemon. I want a new one!" You thrust the laptop into the clerk's hands.

He turns it over, slowly looking at it. Then he looks up at you. "Where's your power cord?" he asks.

"What do you mean? When I bought it they told me I didn't need one. It has a battery."

At this point you can imagine the incredulous look on the salesman's face as he patiently explains that the battery has run dry.

"It's out of juice! You have to recharge it. Go home and plug this thing into a power source!"

In many ways, marriage is a lot like that new laptop. Our marriages might be humming along, but at some point they start to fade, and if we don't take the appropriate measures, they may soon crash. It's easy to think, *Something's wrong with this thing. I need a new one.* But that's not true. You've probably run down your battery, and it's time to plug into a power source.

There's nothing wrong with admitting you need to be plugged in. This is the nature of marriage. You need frequent "charging up" to keep your marriage alive. The recharge in this case doesn't come from an electrical outlet, but something a whole lot more powerful: the spiritual energy supplied by the Holy Spirit. "Be filled with the Spirit," God says to you.

Each of us needs to be connected to the ultimate power Source— God—and then we will be power sources for our marriages as well.

I hope this book will help you recharge your marriage. The Bible says in Genesis 2:24 that when a husband and wife are united, they become "one flesh." I believe this is an ongoing process—it isn't a done deal once we say "I do." In God's eyes, we are one flesh from the moment of marriage, but paradoxically, we must continue becoming one throughout our married lives. Working through this devotional is one way to get plugged into the Source, get connected to each other, and deepen your journey toward becoming one.

I intended this book to be read by couples together, but please don't worry if you are reading it without your spouse's participation. I'm certain that if you put into practice the principles I discuss here, even by yourself, your spiritual life and your marriage will noticeably improve. After all, each of us can work only toward improving ourselves. We can't change our spouses or their behavior. God can do amazing things when we are plugged in to Him.

None of us can be the husband or wife God called us to be without the help and filling of the Spirit. In our own strength, we will utterly fail. It is only as we are continually filled with and yielded to the Spirit that we can be loving husbands and wives in power-filled and powerful marriages.

PONDER

This [Ephesians 5:18] is a command for all Christians. The present tense rules out any once-and-for-all reception of the Spirit but points to a continuous replenishment (literally, "go on being filled"). . . . There may, therefore, be successive fillings of the Spirit; indeed the Christian life should be an uninterrupted filling.

—A. Skevington Wood[1]

PROBE

- What has motivated you to read this book?
- What are you hoping will be the result?

PRAY

Pray that God will fill you with His Spirit and help you make a new commitment to strengthen your marriage. Ask Him for the desire, the will, and the courage to do this.

2

LOVING MAINTENANCE

*Therefore what God has joined together, let man
not separate.*

MATTHEW 19:6

$\mathcal{I}$ know people who get a new computer every year or so. Do you
know anybody like that? Is it you?

It's the same with many of today's hi-tech toys. People want to
have the latest model iPod or Blackberry. Their cell phones double as
cameras and alarm clocks. The televisions are getting bigger and bigger, and now they have flat screens, wide screens, plasma screens, and
who knows what other screens. There is always a better DVD player
you can buy, and of course you have to get one of those portable ones
to watch a movie on an airplane.

Technology these days is advancing so rapidly that by the time
you actually purchase something, it's almost obsolete. Do you realize what this hi-tech culture is doing to us? I think it's training us to
cultivate a mentality that says, "Out with the old, in with the new."
We are living in a society that values whatever is the latest thing or
the up-to-the-minute development. I've heard teenagers talking about
a trend, and they'll groan, "That's *so* five minutes ago." Doesn't that
say it all?

Today's tech culture makes it difficult to appreciate that marriage
works in exactly the opposite way. Like a hand-carved antique clock
or a 1957 Bel Air convertible, the older it is, the more valuable it be-

comes. But—it increases in value only if it is carefully maintained. All of us can choose to turn our marriages into priceless treasures that get better with age. We just have to remember that you don't get treasure by treating it like trash or throwing it out to replace it with the latest model. Loving care is the key.

There is something we can learn, however, from our current hi-tech obsession. What if you bought a beautiful, expensive, top-of-the-line desktop computer and you wanted it to last? Well, the only way that baby is going to keep up with developing software and Internet capabilities is if you continually maintain it, keep your hard drive free of viruses, and occasionally purchase an upgrade for it. You'll still have the same computer, but it will always be "like new."

That's how we need to treat our marriages. We need to keep them in good condition. We need to do regular maintenance and frequently "upgrade." Only instead of increasing our RAM or installing a new operating system, we actively love our spouses, treat them with kindness, constantly think of ways to encourage them, and get to know them better throughout the years. We are careful not to allow "viruses"—destructive influences—into our relationships.

It's a wonderful thing when someone asks how long you've been married and you can give a number in double digits. When people ask me how long I have been married, I tell them, "Thirty-three years."

"Really?" they say, looking at me. Then they look at Cathe and say, "No way! She doesn't look old enough!" (Someone has yet to say that about me!)

Although being married for thirty-three years is rare in today's world, it doesn't have to be. God wants your marriage to last, and He's also given you the Manual on how to accomplish that feat. Best of all, He supplies you with the power to make it happen. He has freely given you everything you need to build your marriage into a treasure. All the maintenance, virus-scanners, and upgrades are free for the asking! If you pay attention to the preservation and protection of your marriage, taking advantage of all the resources God has put at your fingertips, you will not want to chuck the whole thing in favor of the current model. You will soon find that the enticement of whatever is the "latest thing" can't even remotely compare to the value of your lovingly maintained treasure.

PONDER

If we deeply believe that the Lord is able to work on our behalf in all circumstances, then no collection of marital setbacks will prompt us to seriously consider divorce or withdrawal. If God is really as powerful as He claims to be, then the path of obedience will always lead to His intended purposes. The hope (better, the certainty) that God is at work to accomplish His plan even in the most difficult of marriages must remain firmly rooted in our awareness of His powerful grace—and that is Building Block 1.

—Dr. Larry Crabb[2]

PROBE

- Why is it better to lovingly maintain what you already have as opposed to trading it in for a new model?
- What are some maintenance tasks you can perform on your marriage this week?

PRAY

Pray that God will reveal new and creative ways to keep your marriage "like new" and grant you the desire to put them into action.

3

NOT NEW, BUT LIKE NEW

So Jacob served seven years to get Rachel, but they
seemed like only a few days to him because of his
love for her.

GENESIS 29:20

Our culture not only encourages a throwaway mentality about possessions and relationships, it also encourages us to over-romanticize things. Thus the idea of "love at first sight" is a popular notion, underscored by countless idealistic movies, songs, and television programs.

Throughout my years as a pastor, I have spoken with many couples who have just gotten to know each other yet want to rush into marriage. They believe their giddy, thrilling "new love" is enough to make a marriage work. I agree that God gives us this exciting, heightened emotional state at the start of a love relationship to encourage our desire to make the bond permanent. But there's much more to love than the exhilarating feeling of initial romance.

One of my favorite love stories is the one about Jacob and Rachel that begins in Genesis 29. It appears that Jacob experienced something like love at first sight. After he had spent only one month with Rachel's family, his Uncle Laban—Rachel's father—said to him, "Just because you are a relative of mine, should you work for me for nothing? Tell me what your wages should be" (Gen. 29:15). Jacob didn't beat around the bush. He quickly replied, "I'll work for you seven years in return for your younger daughter Rachel" (v. 18).

Laban realized a good bargain when he saw one, so he replied, in essence, "Jacob, I will strike a deal with you. You work for me seven years and you can have my daughter Rachel as your wife."

Jacob agreed, the seven years passed, and at last the long-awaited wedding day arrived. No doubt Jacob felt enormous excitement as he was finally about to consummate his marriage with the beautiful Rachel. Imagine his surprise the next morning when he discovered that the woman lying next to him was actually Rachel's older sister, Leah! As Jacob's eyes adjusted to the morning light, he learned the awful truth. Somehow, Laban had tricked him into marrying the wrong woman. Outraged, Jacob stormed over to his uncle and protested, "Why did you give me Leah? I worked seven years for *Rachel!*"

"We have a custom in our culture," Laban calmly explained, "that you always marry off the older daughter first. If you work for me seven more years, however, you can have Rachel too."

Most men probably would have exploded at such a request and left town in a huff. Not Jacob. He worked seven more years. Do you know why? I think it's because during the seven years he had worked for his Uncle Laban, his breathtaking new love for Rachel had blossomed into a deep, long-lasting dedicated love. Those first seven years "seemed like *only a few days to him* because of his love for her" (emphasis mine). So it was unthinkable that he would give up the hope of marrying her. She was worth another seven years of work—and I'm willing to bet he would have agreed to even more if he'd had to.

That is the kind of love that will last a lifetime—not merely love at first sight. It is when two people have been looking at each other for years that love becomes special. I have been looking at my wife, Cathe, for over three decades now, and she looks better all the time.

Jacob's initial infatuation gave way to committed love—and that is the kind of love that husbands and wives need to cultivate for one another. Let's not waste a precious moment lamenting the loss of our initial romance. Our marriages may not be new, but with the constant filling of the Spirit and loving maintenance, they can always be "like new." Our committed love will be so much deeper, so much more fulfilling and bring us more joy than we ever thought possible. Love at first sight? Sometimes it happens. But love over a lifetime—that's one of the most precious gifts God allows us in this earthly existence.

PONDER

We need to view the wedding ceremony far more seriously than we have. When a man and a woman stand before the minister, they are standing before God, and when they make their vows to each other, they are also making them to God, who will hold us accountable for what we promise. Based on that, we should commit that the word "divorce" will never be uttered with regard to our marriages, for divorce is simply not an option.

—AL JANSSEN[3]

PROBE

- In what ways has the romance in your marriage faded or changed since you and your spouse were first together?
- How would you describe the difference between the initial infatuation and the long-term committed love?

PRAY

Thank God for the initial attraction that brought you and your spouse together, and pray that your marriage will be full of a more solid, long-lasting love that far outshines those early romantic feelings.

4

REALLY LOVE

Husbands, love your wives.
EPHESIANS 5:25

The Bible gives every Christian husband a revolutionary three-word phrase that has the power to radically change any marriage: love your wife. Four times in Ephesians 5:25–33, the apostle Paul reminds men to love their wives.

We husbands tend to gloss over this command, believing that we're already complying with God's instruction. How many times have you heard the story of the woman who asks her husband if he loves her? His answer: "I married you, didn't I?" It doesn't take a brain surgeon to figure out that this is not the answer your wife is looking for.

If each of us were to think through and apply this single command, "Love your wife," it would transform our marriages. Incidentally, it's good advice for women too: love your husband (Titus 2:4).

Now is not the time to concern yourself with what your spouse is doing, whether or not you feel he or she adequately loves you. You focus on what God has called you to do. If you do your part, in most cases your spouse will too. If you begin to really love, most likely your marriage partner will respond in kind.

Does that sound implausible? Think of it this way. Why are you a Christian in the first place? Why is it that you put your faith in Jesus? Probably because God loves you unconditionally. He accepted you as you were—in your ugly, helpless, sinful state—and He began to transform and change you. It was His love that ultimately wore down your rebellion and resistance. The Bible says, "We love because He first loved us" (1 John 4:19).

Our submission to Christ today is a direct result of His love toward us. We have come to see that His plans for us are good. We have come to see that even if God tells us to do something we don't like, it is always for our benefit. So we have learned to surrender to Him. It is difficult at times, but we do it. His love continually wins us over.

The same will be true in a marriage. If a wife can feel confident that her husband has her best interests at heart; if she can see that he loves her so deeply that he continually demonstrates an intense concern for her welfare—then it will be far easier for her to submit to his leadership.

If a husband is certain of his wife's love for him—if he feels respected, admired, and taken care of—then he will be far more likely to be a kind, respectful, and loving leader in the home.

A despairing man once called a friend because his wife was threatening divorce. With resignation in his voice, the dejected man asked his friend to pray for him. His friend said he would but added, "The request I'm going to make in my prayers is that you stop being so acquiescent and fatalistic about all this. You two have had a good marriage—up to now. And a good marriage is worth fighting for."

The man's friend then challenged him to live out the kind of love presented in 1 Corinthians 13. The man accepted his friend's challenge and ultimately saved his marriage.

What did this man do that was so radical? I'm going to point out many ways to love throughout this book, but now I'll just say he did the obvious. He was kind to his wife. He thought of ways to please her. He encouraged her. He refrained from being critical. He listened to her. He demonstrated in obvious ways that he was interested in her. He did all the things one does when we are in the throes of new love. And it worked.

Before we get any further into this journey of becoming one, why not recommit here and now to really love your spouse, today and every day?

PONDER

The call to love is not so much a call to a certain state of feeling as it is to a quality of action. When Paul says, "Love your wives," he is saying, "Be loving toward your wife—treat her as lovely." Do the things that are truly loving things. . . . How are husbands to love their wives? How much love is required of the man? Paul says like Christ loves the Church.

—R. C. SPROUL[4]

PROBE

- Why do you think the apostle Paul thought it necessary to re-iterate the seemingly obvious command "Husbands, love your wives"?
- Using 1 Corinthians 13 as a guide, what are some ways you can love your spouse better today?

PRAY

Ask God for the wisdom to know the best ways to love your spouse.

5

BACK TO THE GARDEN

But you must not eat from the tree of the knowledge of good and evil, for when you eat of it you will surely die.

GENESIS 2:17

In this first section I have been talking about making your marriage "like new." But I want you to know that I'm not looking at marriage through rose-colored glasses. After thirty-three years of it, I'm familiar with the realities. I know there can be rocky times. No marriage, including my own, is without its struggles. And I have spent countless hours talking with couples about their problems as well. Marital strife is nothing new. It goes all the way back to Eden.

Adam and Eve were the perfect couple. Eve was designed and created specifically for Adam, so theirs was an ideal union. We can safely assume they lived in blissful harmony with each other, as with God, the animals, and the land.

But in Genesis 3 we see that Satan, disguised as a serpent, approached Eve in the garden and convinced her to do the one thing God had forbidden. We all know what happened next: "So when the woman saw that the tree was good for food, that it was pleasant to the eyes, and a tree desirable to make one wise, she took of its fruit and ate. She also gave to her husband with her, and he ate. Then the eyes of both of them were opened" (vv. 6–7 NKJV).

Eve was at the wrong place at the wrong time, listening to the wrong voice, which led her to do the wrong thing. Adam soon joined her, and when confronted by God for an explanation of his disobedience, he offered the first excuse recorded in human history: "The woman whom You gave to be with me, she gave me of the tree, and I ate" (v. 12 NKJV).

I don't know what Adam might have emphasized in this response to God. If Adam said, "It's the *woman* You gave me," he was placing the blame on Eve, not himself. On the other hand, if Adam said, "It's the woman *You* gave me," he would have been placing the blame on God Himself. Whatever the case, it was a lame excuse, as Adam was fully responsible for his own actions.

Eve did not do much better as she tried to blame it all on Satan, as though she had nothing to do with it. "The serpent deceived me, and I ate" (v. 13 NKJV). Loose paraphrase: "The devil made me do it."

Standing ashamed in front of God, they were both trying to squirm out of responsibility for their own actions. Can't you just see them glaring at each other as their Creator takes them to task? For the first time ever, a married couple had discord between them. Sin had entered the picture and one of the first things that happened is that marriage became difficult.

Adam and Eve both crossed the line, knowing it was the wrong thing to do. As a result of that sin, a curse came upon humanity, and we feel its repercussions to this very day. Death entered the human race. The curse of sickness, a limited life span, and the ultimate termination of life on Earth began. Dissension between people—husbands and wives, brothers and sisters, parents and children—became the new way of life.

Like sin itself, marital discord started in the garden. So what are we to do? Well, when it comes to sin, we don't just accept it because we've inherited it from our ancestors. We fight against it, and when we fall prey to it, we do our best to repent as soon as possible, ask for forgiveness, and move forward. We should think of marital strife the same way: Try to avoid it. When it happens, resolve it as quickly as possible. Ask and grant forgiveness, and move forward in love.

Like sin, marital strife left unaddressed can have disastrous consequences: disrespect between spouses, emotional distance, and possibly the total demise of the relationship.

What is causing strife between you and your spouse today? Work hard to settle it, for much is at stake. If there are unresolved issues, none of your efforts at making your marriage like new or becoming one will be of any use.

PONDER

Marriage is not a finished affair. No matter to what age you live, love must be continuously consolidated. Being considerate, thoughtful and respectful without ulterior motives is the key to a satisfactory marriage.

—Chinese Pamphlet[5]

PROBE

- Why are marriages so prone to discord?
- What are the most common areas of strife in your marriage, and what are some ideas for changing that pattern?

PRAY

Ask God for the eyes to observe your marital strife head-on and for the humility to confess your part in it and resolve it.

LEAVING AND CLEAVING

This week, focus on learning how to put your marriage above all else except your relationship with God. Ponder the reasons God created marriage in the first place, and praise Him for providing you with a lifelong companion. Consider what it means when Jesus says you are to "leave" father and mother and "cleave" to your spouse.

6

GOD'S DESIGN FOR MARRIAGE

The Lord God said, "It is not good for the man to
be alone. I will make a helper suitable for him."
GENESIS 2:18

Let's go back again to the very beginning, when the whole world
was beautiful and lush. In the middle of this gorgeous world sat the
Garden of Eden. Think of all the amazing places you have ever seen.
Eden surpassed all those. Eden was perfection.

So there was Adam, living in Eden. He had everything that was
"pleasing to the eye" (Gen. 2:9). He was surrounded by the wonders
of God's creation, yet something was still missing from his life. Of
course Adam did not know what it was, because that something was
actually a someone whom God had not yet created. But God knew.
He said, "It is not good for the man to be alone. I will make a helper
suitable for him."

We read again and again in Genesis 1 the phrase "And God saw
that it was good." But when God looked at Adam's loneliness, He
said that it was not good. Why did God bring woman to man? To
provide "a helper suitable for him." This could be translated from the
Hebrew, "someone who assists another to reach fulfillment." This
term appears elsewhere in the Old Testament in reference to someone coming to another's rescue. So Eve came to rescue Adam from
his loneliness.

The account in Scripture says:

The Lord God caused a deep sleep to fall on Adam, and he slept; and He took one of his ribs, and closed the flesh in its place. Then the rib which the Lord God had taken from man He made into a woman, and He brought her to the man. And Adam said,

> "This is now bone of my bones
> And flesh of my flesh;
> She shall be called Woman,
> Because she was taken out of Man." (Genesis 2:21–23 NKJV)

So Adam fell into a deep sleep. Much to his surprise, when he awoke there was Eve! Adam enthusiastically exclaimed, "This is now bone of my bones and flesh of my flesh"! Hebrew experts tell us Adam's reaction was one of thrilling, joyous astonishment. He took a nap, woke up, saw Eve, and said, "Yes! This is good!" Eve was perfect in every way for Adam. She was a partner, someone with whom to share his life.

God brought Adam and Eve together and established marriage: "Therefore shall a man leave his father and his mother, and shall cleave unto his wife: and they shall be one flesh" (Gen. 2:24 KJV). Jesus referenced this same statement in the New Testament. The Pharisees asked Him, "Is it lawful for a man to divorce his wife for just any reason?" Jesus said, "Have you not read that He who made them at the beginning 'made them male and female,' and said, 'For this reason a man shall leave his father and mother and be joined to his wife, and the two shall become one flesh'?" (Matt. 19:3–5 NKJV).

"One flesh." That's pretty profound, isn't it? To me it suggests that to separate a married couple is more complicated than simply signing a few papers and going off in two different directions. It is more akin to actually ripping your body in half. It is ugly and painful and bloody, and the effects can continue forever. Even if, in our current culture, people do not experience that horrific agony upon divorce, it is that way in God's eyes.

God's plan for marriage was that the man and woman would *com-*

plete each other. They would be companions for each other—friends—and they would help each other reach fulfillment in life. They would be each others' helpers and keep each other from loneliness.

Let's focus on this basic description of marriage. Try to look beyond the daily hassles, like bill paying, child rearing, and juggling careers. Look back at God's original intention for your married life: Friendship. Companionship. Help. Protection from loneliness. Security. When you look at it this way, doesn't marriage seem simple?

PONDER

A successful marriage requires falling in love many times, always with the same person.

— Mignon McLaughlin[6]

PROBE

- How well are you living up to God's basic plan for marriage?
- Why are we so easily distracted from these basics?

PRAY

Give God thanks for His creation of marriage and for giving you a lifelong companion. Ask Him to guide you in the ways you need to get back to the basics.

7

YOU CAN'T CLEAVE TILL YOU LEAVE

*For this reason a man will leave his father and
mother and be united to his wife.*

MATTHEW 19:5

$\mathcal{M}$atthew 19 provides some essential truths regarding God's design for marriage. In fact, two words sum it up: leaving and cleaving. First you leave. Then you cleave.

Marriage begins with a leaving—of all other relationships. Ironically, Adam and Eve did not have to leave any other relationships, since they had none except that with God. But in the future, they would have to heed this command in keeping their marital relationship primary, ahead of the relationships with their children and their descendants.

We are to leave all other relationships, at least in their present state. Of course, we are still sons or daughters to our parents, but the relationship is different. A new family has been established. A man's primary commitment, once he is married, is to his wife, and her primary commitment is to him.

These days, many people are waiting until they are a little older to get married. By the time they are in their late twenties or early thirties, they've usually established a new "family." They have a tight circle of friends with whom they do nearly everything. They are comfortable with this lifestyle. Still, when they get married, they are required to "leave" these friends, in the sense that this group can no longer be primary in their lives. The new spouse must be number one. This can be a difficult adjustment.

What happens in some marriages is that the process of leaving never takes place. One or both parties think, *If things don't work out, I can always run home to my parents,* or *If things don't work out, I'm going to run back to my old friends and hang out with them.* People who think this way have never really left their other relationships and haven't chosen to cleave to their spouses. Husband, your best friend and closest confidante in life needs to be your wife. Wife, the same needs to be true for you. It is good to have other friends, but you should have only one best friend in your life, and it should be your spouse.

It becomes especially dangerous when a wife has male friends other than her husband, and a husband has female friends other than his wife. You see, the problem is that you start bonding with these people. It can easily lead to greater friendship, and even intimacy and possibly adultery.

Most adulterous relationships do not begin with sexual attraction. In fact, they start rather innocently. They begin because a married person feels his or her spouse isn't providing enough attention. So the person develops a friendship with someone of the opposite sex. "We're just friends," this person says. "It's nothing more. We encourage one another. We're like soul mates. We even have prayer together." Believe it or not, these can easily become famous last words.

Husband, make your wife your best friend. Wife, make your husband your best friend. Cultivate the friendship in your marriage. After all, that was God's master plan for marriage from the very beginning: companionship.

Listen to what God said in Malachi 2:14: "It is because the LORD is acting as the witness between you and the wife of your youth, because you have broken faith with her, though she is your partner, the wife of your marriage covenant." Notice the words "partner" and "wife." That word "partner" could be translated from the Hebrew to say, "one with whom you are united in thoughts, goals, plans, and efforts." Is that a good description of your present relationship with your spouse? If not, it ought to be.

So, first you leave. Every other relationship in your life must work in proportion to the relationship between you and your spouse. There is a place for buddies. There is a place for hobbies. There is a place for your career. There is a place for your parents, and of course, a place for your children. But you shouldn't let anything get in the way of your relationship with your spouse. That is all a part of the leaving process.

A word of caution: if somehow you find yourself in an abusive relationship where there was the threat of physical harm to you or your children, that supercedes the scenario I have described. But under normal circumstances, your marriage should come before everything else in your life—with the obvious exception of God Himself.

PONDER

The principle of "leaving" parents is also important in decision making. Your parents may have suggestions about many aspects of your married life. Each suggestion should be taken seriously, but, in the final analysis, you must make your own decision. You should no longer make decisions on the basis of what would make parents happy but on the basis of what would make your partner happy. Under God, you are a new unit, brought together by His Spirit to live for each other (Phil. 2:3–4).

—Dr. Gary Chapman[7]

PROBE

- What could be the harm in maintaining close primary relationships with parents, siblings, or friends once you are married?
- Are there any relationships in your life that are infringing on your marriage? What should you do about them?

PRAY

Ask God if He sees any relationships in your life that need to change so that your marriage can thrive. Seek His wisdom about how to handle them.

8

CHOOSING WHAT IS BETTER

Mary has chosen what is better, and it will not be taken away from her.

LUKE 10:42

The idea of *leaving* brings with it some serious choices. You have to reprioritize, put things in a different hierarchy in your life. We've talked about the necessity to "leave" your other relationships. But what is the one relationship that many American men, and some women, are most likely to hang on to?

It's their work.

We can all think of a million reasons why our jobs need to be our number-one priority: *It's my responsibility to support the family. The company is counting on me. If I don't work these extra hours I could lose my job. If I don't agree to frequent travel I won't get the raise or the promotion. At work I am needed . . . valued . . . respected. At work nobody nags me to take out the garbage.*

Or even better: *It's my calling. It's God's will. It's what God wants me to do with my life.*

Every one of those statements may have some element of truth in it. But none of them acknowledges the importance of your marriage as the priority in your life, second only to your relationship with God.

If you're like me, you're probably overwhelmed with the sheer volume of things to do, places to go, and people to meet in your daily life. The idea of trying to "balance" your marriage, family, and work is laughable. It's more like a juggling act, and you're barely keeping the balls in the air. So when someone says you must "leave" all that and "cleave" to your spouse, it sounds like just one more thing on your already impossible to-do list.

Jesus has seen this dilemma before. You remember the story of Mary and Martha in Luke 10. Martha rushed around, dizzy with the work and preparations, while Mary sat at the feet of Jesus listening to His teaching. Jesus gently reminded Martha that there was something better than her busyness: time spent with Him. That's what He reminds us too: time spent with Him is the most important time of all. We need to choose it.

This lesson can also apply to God's intentions for us in marriage. We need to *choose what is better*, on a daily basis.

Work is good.

A thriving marriage is better.

A dynamic walk with the Lord is best.

When you have a choice, choose what is better. The best part is that if you are in a vibrant relationship with God and trusting Him every step of the way, He will honor your choice. He will not let your family starve if you sometimes need to forsake your work in order to tend to your marriage.

You may be a God-fearing person with intense loyalty and high moral standards. You'd *never* be unfaithful to your spouse. But make sure you are not being "unfaithful" through excessive devotion to your work. You cannot be one flesh with someone if you are rarely in the same room, if you never spend time alone together, or if you barely know each other.

Think about how much time you spend at work. Forty, fifty, sixty hours a week? Now estimate how many hours you spend with your spouse. Count everything: doing chores or shopping together, meals, family time, fun time, everything. I'd guess the maximum is about thirty hours a week. But when you subtract the time each of you participates in nonwork activities outside the home, and the time each of you spends in the home but not together, that number is getting pretty small, isn't it? Likely you spend only twenty, ten, or even five hours a week with your mate. Compare that to fifty hours on the job! Can you see why I'm being so adamant about this? It's urgently important to pay attention and not let your working hours get out of hand.

At some point you have to leave. So you can cleave.

PONDER

The way our society and our work environments are currently structured, we give the least time to those we value most. If we are wise, we will understand that success as defined by the world isn't success. Success in God's eyes is measured by love. One day He will push the delete button, wiping out all the time clocks, bank statements, productivity sheets, and 401k plans. All that will be left is love. And when love judges the universe, it will be transparently clear: family matters.

—Richard A. Swenson, MD[8]

PROBE

- In what ways does your work interfere with your married life?
- What are some specific steps you can take to prioritize your marriage over your work?

PRAY

Express your thanks for the profitable work that God brings you, and ask Him to show you how to keep it properly prioritized in your life.

9

DON'T LEAVE UNTIL YOU CAN CLEAVE

*Therefore shall a man leave his father and his
mother, and shall cleave unto his wife: and they
shall be one flesh.*

GENESIS 2:24 (KJV)

$\mathcal{I}$t is no use leaving unless you are willing to spend a lifetime
cleaving. The word used in Genesis 2:24 for "cleave" is sometimes
translated as "be united to" or "be joined to" and means "to adhere
to, to stick to, to be attached by some strong tie." You might be thinking, *That's me, all right. I'm stuck.* But that is not what this word means.
In the verb form, it speaks of something that is done aggressively,
a determined action. It is not talking about merely being stuck together, but it is the idea of holding on to something. In other words,
it is not that you are just held to something, like a fly on flypaper,
wanting to get loose. It is that you are choosing to strongly hold onto
something.

For example, say you were walking along the edge of a cliff and
suddenly lost your footing. As you slipped over the side, if you somehow managed to grab a branch, you would cling to that branch for
your very life. In other words, it would be something you chose to
do. That is the idea of the word "cleave" here: it is not that you are
"stuck" to your spouse but that you are aggressively holding on, because your marriage and union depend on it.

This is what needs to happen in our marriages. There are so many pressures on us to be pulled apart. We need to make a determined effort to hold on to one another and to stay away from anything or anyone that would separate us.

The New Testament use of the same word in the Greek language means "to cement together, to stick like glue, or to be welded together so the two cannot be separated without serious damage to both." Therefore, we must periodically take stock and ask ourselves, *Is there any pursuit in which I'm currently involved that puts distance between my mate and me? Is this thing that I am doing drawing us together or is it driving us apart?*

It is not always the big things that bring a marriage down. Certainly there are big issues, such as unfaithfulness or abuse, that can destroy a marriage quickly. But often it is the little things. As Song of Solomon says, it is "the little foxes that spoil the vines" (2:15 NKJV). In a marriage, it can be a matter of neglecting the principle of cleaving. When you are unwilling to hold on tightly to your spouse, your marriage can begin to weaken. Problems can develop. You may transfer the affection you should have for your mate to someone else. So cleave to your spouse and recognize that all other relationships must be secondary.

It is easier than you think to lose that grip on your spouse. I'm not talking only about sinful extramarital relationships, but what we might classify as the "good" ones. You may have an amazing best friend who is the same sex as you. You're close, and you may have been friends for longer than you've known your spouse. Remember what they say about too much of a good thing! Don't let that great friendship interfere with your marriage. Work to make sure it remains the blessing that God intends it to be.

All other relationships must be evaluated in the light of your relationship with your spouse. As I said before, make him or her your best friend. Start communicating with each other as never before. Hold on to each other purposely instead of thinking passively, *We're married. I suppose we'll stick together.* Make conscious choices. For example, when something exciting happens, choose to call your spouse first instead of your mother or your best friend. Actively reach out to him or her, especially when you have the choice to reach out to someone else. As you aggressively do your part, following the counsel of Scripture, God will do His part, and He will bless your home.

Leave and cleave: these are two key words in a successful marriage.

PONDER

That's when it occurred to me. *I am stuck with [my dog] Liz.* The courtship was over, and the honeymoon had ended. We were mutually leashed. Liz went from an option to an obligation, from a pet to a chore, from someone to play with to someone to care for. . . . I discovered that this condition is a common malady known as *stuckititis*.

—MAX LUCADO[9]

PROBE

- What factors in your life challenge your ability or desire to cleave to your mate?
- What can you do when you get an attack of "stuckititis"—when you're resigned to being "stuck" but not excited about aggressively holding on?

PRAY

Ask God to show you what it means to actively hold on to your spouse, and promise Him you will do it.

10

KISS YOUR HUSBAND FIRST

May your fountain be blessed,
and may you rejoice in the wife of your youth.
PROVERBS 5:18

$\mathcal{A}$ wise woman related a simple story that captured the idea of cleaving:

One of the most profound sentiments I've yet heard on marriage came from my good friend Lisa. Before either of us were married, we were riding bikes along the beach one gorgeous Sunday. Stopping for a sip of water, we watched a rather tender scene unfold as a mom walked up to join her family, where clearly Dad and their two kids had been playing for some time. Newly arriving on the scene, the mom ran to her children, embraced them with a big bear hug, audible kisses and joyful peals of laughter—and the three frolicked off to look at the sand castle the kids had constructed. Several minutes later, she walked back and greeted her husband.

While I was pulled vicariously into this happy exchange, Lisa had a different take. She shook her head rather woefully and said, "Lady, kiss your husband first."

That's all we said on the subject, but those words have echoed back to me many times over the years. I can still see that husband standing as an outsider to the picture in which he should have been central. My remembering to "kiss my husband first" keeps our marriage rightfully at the core of our family. My husband and I know that the best gift we can give our daughters, in addition to the love and care we extend to them, is to love one another first.

Kiss your husband first. Kiss your wife first. Those words perfectly express the way we are to cleave to our spouses. This is another way of saying "Rejoice in your marriage." When we rejoice in our marriages, we can't help but cleave. Notice that Proverbs 5:18 relates "rejoicing" in your spouse to being "blessed." Yes, it is indeed a blessing when we can rejoice, enjoy, celebrate, and delight in our marriages.

Sometimes I think our modern culture makes it more difficult than ever for us to cleave in our marriages. For one thing, we are surrounded by so many people all the time. If we need help, a listening ear, or someone with whom to see a movie, there are usually people around to satisfy our desires. We don't necessarily need our spouses for that.

For another thing, cleaving seems to imply some type of dependence—and that's a dirty word in our society! We value our *independence*. That's what America is all about. It's a free country! So the idea of cleaving—which sounds ominously like *clinging*—might seem distasteful to modern-day Westerners.

At the risk of being politically incorrect, another of our hurdles is that the women's movement of the 1970s led to some distorted views about relationships. While career opportunities opened up for women during those times, and long-standing myths about women's inferiority were shattered, some new myths became part of our culture. In particular, I'm talking about the myth that "a woman needs a man the way a fish needs a bicycle." This belief certainly makes it difficult for women to accept the idea of holding on aggressively to their husbands. The truth is, men and women *need each other*. In marriage our need for each other is both fulfilled and intensified.

What this means is that once again, as Christians we have to swim against the cultural tide in order to do what is right. Our culture says, *Do what you want.* God says, *Cleave to your mate.* Our culture says, *You are independent.* God says, *You are not, and you never were.* We need to persistently choose to place our marriages ahead of everything else, leaving behind all others and cleaving to our spouses. Wives, kiss your husband first. And husbands, kiss your wives first. It's simple. But it works.

PONDER

Then I did the simplest thing in the world. I leaned down . . . and kissed him. And the world cracked open.

—AGNES DE MILLE[10]

PROBE

- List the ways that your work, your friends, your children, and your activities hinder you from fully cleaving to your mate.
- What do you think would happen if, from now on, you made it a habit to always kiss your spouse first?

PRAY

Ask God to open your eyes to any beliefs you hold that might be hindering you from properly cleaving.

13

POSITIVE COMMUNICATION

Everyone knows that communication is important in marriage. We're going to take a closer look at some aspects of everyday communication: listening, understanding, knowing how to speak our spouse's language, and avoiding anger. Pay special attention this week to the ways you and your spouse communicate, and think about ways you could grow closer together by communicating more effectively.

11

QUICK TO LISTEN

My dear brothers and sisters, be quick to listen,
slow to speak, and slow to get angry.

JAMES 1:19 (NLT)

We have spent a week thinking specifically about our words. Now I want to broaden this concept and talk about communication in general. When you ask married people the secret of a good relationship, often they will say "communication" without even thinking. We all know communication is important, but when pressed to explain what it really means, we all have different answers.

"Communication means talking to each other a lot."

"It means resolving your problems without fighting."

"Communication is staying in touch throughout the day."

I'd like to focus a little more clearly on ways to communicate in marriage, and the first thing I want to talk about is *listening*. James 1:19 is a verse I think we should post where we can see it on a daily basis. Too often we are swift to speak and slow to listen. But James is saying, "Take the time to hear what's being said."

Have you ever made a statement to your spouse or your children based on an incorrect understanding of what was happening, because you didn't take the time to hear the person out? You made a snap judgment. The Bible says, "What a shame, what folly, to give advice before listening to the facts!" (Prov. 18:13 NLT). In our time of instant messaging and ten-second sound bites, we find it hard to slow down, be still, and listen. But we need to be quick to hear what our husbands or wives have to say.

I like to communicate with Cathe throughout my day. I call her up, tell her what's going on, and bring her up to speed. When I'm on a trip, I call her and tell her about some experiences that I've had, and I am amazed at how much she remembers. Later, we'll be visiting with someone, and she will start telling a story that I told her. As she describes it, it is so vivid and accurate, I think, *Was she there with me?* After thirty-three years of marriage, she knows what I mean when I say certain words. She discerns things by the tone of my voice. Cathe is "quick to hear," and that is vitally important in a marriage.

I think the reason Cathe is so good at understanding and remembering what I'm saying is that she's an active listener. It comes naturally to her, but not to most of us— certainly not to me! (I'm more of the "talk until somebody stops me" type.)

Many communication experts have written books and articles about the techniques of active listening. I don't want to make it too complicated, so I'll just relate a couple of key concepts I've learned:

- The point of active listening is *not* to agree with the speaker but to *understand* what he or she is saying.
- The hallmark of active listening is completely focusing on the speaker, being careful not to let your mind wander, and especially avoiding trying to formulate a response in your mind while the person is still speaking.
- Active listening involves periodically clarifying that you understand by offering your interpretation. This gives the speaker a chance to correct you if your understanding is wrong.

In a conversation with your spouse, pay attention to what he or she is saying—not what's going on around you. If you're talking in person (as opposed to on the telephone), don't look at the clock, try to maintain eye contact. Occasionally, reflect back what you thought you heard. Active listening and frequent clarifying will go a long way

toward great communication in your marriage. Let's be quick to listen and slow to speak.

PONDER

But often when women tell men, "You aren't listening," and the men protest, "I am," the men are right. . . . I found that at every age, the girls and women faced each other directly, their eyes anchored on each other's faces. At every age, the boys and men sat at angles to each other and looked elsewhere in the room, periodically glancing at each other. They were obviously attuned to each other, often mirroring each other's movements. But the tendency of men to face away can give women the impression they aren't listening even when they are.

—DEBORAH TANNEN[11]

PROBE

- What issues have arisen in your marriage that have to do with listening? How did you resolve them?
- List some ways you could increase your active listening skills, and begin to put them into practice this week.

PRAY

Ask God to help you be a good listener today.

12

SHE SAYS—HE HEARS

But blessed are your eyes because they see, and
your ears because they hear.

MATTHEW 13:16

When there is a breakdown in communication, it begins to hurt the marriage. One husband was overheard saying to his wife, "Honey, what do you mean, we don't communicate? Just yesterday I e-mailed you a reply to the message you left on my voice mail!" That's twenty-first-century communication for you.

Still, it's amazing how a husband and wife who are trying to communicate can talk past each other. What a wife says may translate into something entirely different for her husband. Likewise, what he says may mean something else to his wife. When a couple driving somewhere get lost, she'll say, "Let's ask for directions." But he hears, "You're not a man."

When she says, "Can I have the remote control?" he hears, "Let's watch something that will bore you beyond belief!"

She says, "I would like to redecorate."

He hears, "Let's take our money and flush it down the toilet."

She tells him, "You need to get in touch with your feelings."

He hears, "Blah, blah, blah."

She asks, "Are you listening to me?"

He hears, "Blah, blah, blah."

What we have here is a failure to communicate because of our differences as men and women, and our differences as individuals. We often interpret what was said in light of our own preconceptions, and we entirely miss the point. That's why active listening is so important. For example, Cathe might tell me, "Please don't have another cookie." I could feel hurt and go off sulking, thinking she was insulting me. But if I spoke up and asked her, "Are you saying I need to lose some weight?" she might say, "No, it's just that I'm saving them for my women's group tonight." And what could have become a problem between us has been avoided.

However, we sometimes have communication snags not because of a wrong interpretation, but because we weren't listening well and didn't clearly hear what was said. One man tells the story of how he nearly walked away from his engagement to the woman he's been married to for sixteen years:

> We were working on a yearbook project, putting photos together with names and descriptions. At one point she asked me if Kari had been involved in a certain program. I told her, no; Gary could not have been involved in that program because he was somewhere else at the time. She said she was sure Kari had been there. I insisted it wasn't possible. We argued for some time until I finally pushed myself away from the table and told her firmly (in a voice that could be construed as shouting), "I know I'm right!"
>
> I left and took a walk. I reconsidered every aspect of our relationship. I seriously thought she had lost her mind. How could someone I cared about be so hardheaded and refuse to listen to me? I knew I was right about the situation and thought that if she couldn't admit it, it was probably better that I'd found out now and not later. I returned to the house and we did not say a word to each other for a couple of hours. Finally I sat down with her, and said in a clear, calm voice, "There is no way that Gary Jones could have been there because he was with me at the time." She stared at me in stunned silence, then said, "Of course not. Kari Smith was there because Gary was somewhere else."
>
> I honestly don't remember the rest of the conversation, only that we were blown away at how close we came to destroying the relationship simply because we weren't listening to one another. Ever since

then, the lesson that has been dearest to my heart is that marriage isn't just about communication . . . it's about *clear* communication.

This man was fortunate that he learned so early the importance of speaking clearly and making sure he understood what his spouse was saying. If we don't, we can hurt each other's feelings, convey misinformation, and even seriously damage the relationship.

PONDER

Why such a high priority on communication? Because good communication is the key to what all of us who marry basically want . . . to love and be loved. We want to share our lives with someone who loves us unconditionally. We want to grow old with a mate who has valued us, understood us, and helped us feel safe in sharing our deepest feelings and needs. We want to make love last forever. And this type of loving relationship is most often attained by couples who have learned how to reach the deepest levels of verbal intimacy.

—GARY SMALLEY[12]

PROBE

- Think of times you and your mate were speaking past each other. Can you identify any situations or topics in which this is most likely to happen?
- What are your ideas for avoiding this type of miscommunication in your marriage?

PRAY

Ask that you clearly hear God's voice and that in staying close to Him, you will have the grace to speak and listen effectively in your marriage.

13

SPEAK HIS/HER LANGUAGE

*In the past God spoke to our forefathers through
the prophets at many times and in various ways,
but in these last days he has spoken to us by his
Son.*

HEBREWS 1:1–2

Throughout history, God has spoken to individuals in ways He knew they would hear and understand. Jacob, Mary, and others were visited by angels. Pharaoh, Joseph (Jacob's son), and Joseph (Mary's husband) received messages from God through their dreams. Balaam had the distinction of hearing God's voice through a talking donkey, while Jonah had to be swallowed by a fish before he really listened to the Lord. A few have heard God's voice speaking directly to them: Abraham, Moses, and Paul, to name a few.[13]

Following God's example, we need to do everything possible to understand our spouses and speak to them in ways they can "get." We can't just speak—we have to speak and act in such a way that we know our spouses will hear. This means we must develop, over the years, a very intimate knowledge of our spouses so that our communication improves over time.

Forgive me for generalizing here, but in many ways, men and women speak different languages. Men tend to prefer "just the facts, ma'am," while women love to speak about their thoughts and feelings. Men generally communicate in order to give and receive information; women converse because they want to *relate*. I often hear men say that it drives them crazy that women need to talk so much. And it really irritates women that men never want to "talk about their feelings." Men are more goal-oriented while women tend to be more relationship-oriented. Simply acknowledging these differences, along with getting to know the particular communication style of your mate, can go a long way toward improving your marriage.

One of the complaints I hear from women is that they want their husbands to *listen* to them—not jump in and try to solve their problems. But it's not always true. If Cathe is telling me about the clogged toilet, you can bet she doesn't just want me to listen to her feelings about it! This can be confusing. How do we know when to solve the problem and when to just listen? We should get in the habit of using our discernment in these situations, and when in doubt, just ask.

I heard about one husband who listens to his wife talk about all the problems and obstacles she's facing at work, and at some point, he'll ask (with a touch of humor in his voice), "Is this one of those times you just want me to listen, or would you like some ideas for solving this problem?" His wife loves that he does this, and it gives her the opportunity to clarify what she wants. She will often realize, to her own surprise, that she indeed would like his help. But had he offered it without asking, she may have been offended.

When women talk with each other, they tend to tell long, involved stories with a point or punch line buried somewhere near the end. I guess women enjoy the process of storytelling and listening for the ending. However, when women try to use this formula in speaking with their husbands, it can end in frustration for both parties. The husband is anxious for a point, and the wife is angry that he doesn't seem to be listening. Wives, if you want to capture your husbands' attention, I suggest you consider this one simple rule: *lead with your best stuff*. In other words, begin with the punch line. You'll grab his interest and he's likely to listen as you explain all the important details.

When Jesus was walking around teaching, He always used examples His listeners could relate to. He taught using metaphors such as soil, fishing, sowing and harvesting, servants and slaves, sheep, and fig trees. He was speaking the language of the people He wanted to teach. Imagine if Jesus were walking around today—I wonder if some of his parables would mention cell phones, laptops, and iPods? Let's do our best to speak our spouses' languages. You might be amazed at the new level of harmony in your marriage.

PONDER

You and your mate have enormous differences, and no amount of work can bridge that gap. As a result, you have to learn to manage your relationship despite the differences. What's more, you need to embrace those differences, find value in them. Resisting the differences by being judgmental about them will cause you nothing but pain. . . . God didn't design us to be the same, he designed us to be different.

—DR. PHILLIP C. McGRAW[14]

PROBE

- List some differences between you and your mate in communication styles. At what times do these disparities become most obvious?
- What ways have you found to effectively bridge these communication gaps?

PRAY

Thank God for the uniqueness with which He has created every individual. Praise Him especially for your spouse and ask for the wisdom to continue growing in your understanding of him/her.

14

IT'S ABOUT CONNECTING

Let the peace of Christ rule in your hearts, since as
members of one body you were called to peace.
COLOSSIANS 3:15

Have you noticed lately how many issues you and your mate legitimately disagree about? Sometimes it can be disconcerting to realize that no matter how much we love each other, Cathe and I are simply not going to have the same outlook on everything in life. How do we maintain peace in our families while being true and authentic with each other, in spite of differing viewpoints?

As a male in our society, I was raised with the notion that the goal of everything was always to *win*. Consequently, I started off marriage thinking it was my duty to convince Cathe that she needed to agree with me whenever we differed, and I thought the conversation couldn't be over until I'd won. Fortunately for our marriage, I've come to realize that the point of marital communication is not to agree, but to connect. All of our interaction should have as its goal a closer relationship, a deeper oneness.

I think most of us believe that problem-solving skills are paramount to a healthy marriage, and that we need to be good at resolving our differences. But we are never going to resolve our deep disagreements. Healthy couples find a way to coexist in disagreement. They agree to disagree without using those words or even realizing they are doing it.

I've found that the differences between husband and wife can make for wonderful conversations. One woman said, "I finally decided that rather than berate my husband for his compulsive need to participate in sports and his inability to sit still, I would start trying to understand it. I began asking him questions that allowed him to open up about it. He couldn't believe I was interested! These discussions were not only fascinating, they helped me know my husband better and they showed him that I really cared about who he is. I may not ever be able to relate on a personal level—I'm more of the homebody-bookworm type—but I have a new appreciation for the uniqueness of my man."

The next time the two of you are facing a disagreement, try to pull back before it turns into a debate. Find some common ground. Acknowledge that the first priority is your relationship, and you don't have to agree on everything. See if you can find a way to accept that you disagree. Move toward the goal of *peace*, which is different from *resolution*.

Jesus told the disciples, "Peace I leave with you; my peace I give you. I do not give to you as the world gives. Do not let your hearts be troubled and do not be afraid" (John 14:27). His parting gift was peace—that is what God wants for us in our marriages. Let's do our best to communicate with the goal of peace.

PONDER

I don't care how different a husband and wife are, it's possible to learn to adjust, to adapt, to live in peace and harmony, to be compatible. I've seen it happen. One of the delights of counseling is to see . . . those who have been married for thirty years discover how to understand, accept, adjust to, and honor their partners' uniquenesses.

—H. Norman Wright[15]

PROBE

- Why is it sometimes so difficult to accept that nobody is going to win an argument?
- What are some consistent areas of disagreement in your marriage, and what can you do to minimize or eliminate conflict in this area?

PRAY

Ask God to give you peace in times of stress and disagreement.

15

SLOW TO ANGER

For man's anger does not bring about the righteous
life that God desires.

JAMES 1:20

We discussed earlier that we should be slow to speak and quick to listen. James also tells us we should be slow to get angry. As Proverbs 29:11 tells us, "A fool gives full vent to anger, but a wise person quietly holds it back" (NLT). Don't let anger control your life. Don't let it have a place in your marriage.

I heard about newlyweds who decided to put into practice Ephesians 4:26, which says, "'Be angry, and do not sin': do not let the sun go down on your wrath" (NKJV). So they determined never to go to bed mad at each other. Thirty years later, someone asked the husband how it worked out. He said, "Pretty well, but sometimes it was a little rough sitting up all night."

Some people have a hard time disagreeing without getting angry. They feel personally slighted if their spouses have different perspectives on something. They feel an urgent need for resolution, and it needs to be resolved their way! Their anger is often out of proportion to the size of the issue. The problem is, people who are often angry become bitter and they are certainly hard to live with.

If you or your spouse fit this description, beware. Bitterness will infect your marriage and can also spread to your children and to others in your life. The Bible warns about a root of bitterness that can spring up and "defile many" (Heb. 12:15). Don't let bitterness overtake your marriage.

Have you been wronged by your spouse? Are you having a hard time accepting a differing opinion your mate holds? Has he or she hurt you? The key is to forgive him or her. "But he [she] doesn't deserve it," you say. Regardless of what someone has said or done to us, the Bible tells us, "And be kind to one another, tenderhearted, forgiving one another, even as God in Christ forgave you" (Eph. 4:32 NKJV).

There will always be disagreements in marriage. How can we argue constructively, without bitterness or anger creeping in? In other words, what are some ways to "fight fair"? Here are a few ideas:

- Never argue in front of your children, neighbors, friends, or extended family members. Keep your disagreements private.
- Stay focused on the topic at hand. Don't bring up a previous argument, all your spouse's faults, or another subject entirely. If one of you does this, the other should call him or her on it.
- Avoid name-calling and generalities, such as "I can't believe how stubborn you are!" Do your best to talk about the subject at hand and do not call into question each other's character.
- Don't be afraid to take a time-out to calm down. You may both need it sometimes, but make sure this doesn't turn into a convenient way to ignore the problem.
- If you are going to let it go and agree to disagree, acknowledge this so that it doesn't feel like an open wound. Say something like, "It doesn't look as if I'm going to convince you of my perspective, and I don't think I'm going to agree with yours. Can we let this go for now?"
- If you are feeling angry and may lose control, take a break. Examine your anger. It is usually something else in disguise: a hurt, a fear, an anxiety. Your discussion will be more effective if you can be more authentic.

Most importantly, make it a point to reconnect after a disagreement. Praying together is one way, and I know many of you have another very nice way of "making up." Forgive each other, just as God has extended forgiveness to you. When you forgive someone, you set a prisoner free: *yourself.* Let it go. Forgive. Put it behind you. Don't carry it any farther. Being slow to anger and quick to forgive can be one of the best gifts you give your marriage.

PONDER

Remember that you are trying to grow together. Often we learned unhealthy or unfair ways of fighting from parents or from our culture. These make winning at any cost the most important goal. If one spouse wins . . . both lose.

—Gerald Foley[16]

PROBE

- To what extent do you and your spouse express anger in your marriage? Has this changed over time?
- What techniques work for you in diffusing anger between you and your mate? What are some other things you could try?

PRAY

Ask that God would protect both you and your spouse from bitterness, resentment, and unresolved anger.

THE MEANING OF COMMITMENT

As we focus on understanding commitment this week, take time to reflect on what your vows mean to you. Has your appreciation of commitment changed during the time you've been married? Spend this week focusing on the commitment in your own heart—toward God and your spouse—and evaluating its strength. Is your covenant solid? Or could it use some shoring up?

16

MY MARRIAGE SECRET

A woman is bound to her husband as long as he lives.

1 CORINTHIANS 7:39

People have often asked me to reveal the secret to a successful marriage. In my case, the answer is that I married Cathe. But since you can't do that, let's consider a bedrock principle that everyone can apply to his or her own marital relationship.

When Cathe and I got married, we heeded the advice of Benjamin Franklin, who once said, "Keep your eyes wide open before marriage, half shut afterwards."[17] We also took our time. We courted for three years. We endured big, dramatic breakups that seemed to become annual events—the type of breakups where we said, "I never want to see your face again. It is over with!" But it wasn't over with, because whether we knew it or not, in our hearts we had already committed ourselves to one another.

And that's the secret: commitment.

As Cathe and I spent time apart, our love only grew. That's not always the case in relationships, so it was a good sign. Eventually I began to realize that she was the only girl for me. And more than three decades later, we're still a happy couple.

I can remember our wedding day as though it happened yesterday. A vision of beauty, walking gracefully down the aisle, took my breath away. I, on the other hand, looked like mountain man Jeremiah

Johnson, just in from the woods. I had a bushy red beard and long hair, parted in the middle and reaching to my shoulders. Underneath all that hair, however, my wife could see that there was . . . a bald man in the making! Nevertheless, on that wonderful day, we publicly made our commitment to each other official.

I believe every couple should be able to look each other in the eye and say, "Being *divorced* is not an option." This can be scary, but you need to be brutally honest with yourself about it. If you can't say it *and mean it*, and you are already married, then I recommend you do everything possible to work on yourself and your marriage until you *can* say it. This could include marital counseling and/or individual counseling (and I suggest you find a Christian counselor), pastoral counseling, a marriage group at your church, a mentoring relationship with a Godly older couple, or simply praying about it daily and working it through with God and your spouse.

Please hear me when I say you cannot pretend about this. You can't say "I am committed to you forever" and just hope that someday it will be true. If it's not true right this minute, you must address it, or you will be in for some rough and painful times in the future.

Wedlock should be a padlock. Getting married should be as permanent and secure as turning a lock and throwing away the key. Marriage means standing by the commitment we have made, come what may. This is not only God-honoring, it's practical. Once you are secure in the relationship, you and your spouse are free to negotiate disagreements and weather rocky times without fearing that one of you will leave. You should have a pact that whatever the issue is at stake, no matter how significant or how strongly you disagree, *the marriage itself is never at stake*.

Such an attitude prompts me to think of a statement made by Winston Churchill in a 1940 speech: "We shall fight on the beaches. We shall fight on the landing grounds. We shall fight in the fields, and in the streets, we shall fight in the hills. We shall never surrender!"[18] He held his ground even when the Nazis began bombing London day and night. Evacuation—quitting—was not an option.

We need that same attitude in marriage. Sure, the bombs will drop. Of course the problems will come. But despite the inevitable struggles, we need to say, "We are going to make it. We are not evacuating. We are going to stick this out. And we will prevail."

Marriage is all about commitment. And there is no secret greater than that.

PONDER

If our confidence in God's grace is sufficient to maintain hope when despair seems justified, then we are in a position to commit ourselves to doing whatever God says. We can act on the strength of our hope by persisting to work on our marriages even when tempted to quit.

—Dr. Larry Crabb[19]

PROBE

- Examine the depth and strength of your own marital commitment. How do you keep it strong even when you don't feel like it?
- Why does the day-to-day function of your marriage run more smoothly if the two of you are confident of your commitment?

PRAY

Ask that you would be persevering in your commitment, not in your own strength but in God's. Ask the Lord to help you increase your loyalty to your vow.

17

DISCOVERING GOD'S WILL

*You need to persevere so that when you have done
the will of God, you will receive what he has
promised.*

HEBREWS 10:36

$\mathcal{B}$efore we're married, most of us do a lot of wondering about whether this girlfriend or that boyfriend might turn out to be "God's will" for us—that is, whether we might be dating our future spouses.

My friend's wife tells about the time she was on the second or third date with her now-spouse. As she watched him, she suddenly thought, *Am I looking at my future husband?* Over the next several months of dating, she pondered that question more rigorously. *Could it be God's will for me to marry this man?*

Once she decided that the answer was yes, she also said yes to his proposal of marriage. And now they're both enjoying God's will for their lives. For them, the question of "Is this the right one?" has been settled forever—regardless of the problems they may yet have to face.

How could God make His will any more plain? "I hate divorce," He says in Malachi 2:16. "So guard yourself in your spirit, and do not break faith." Instead of spending any time wondering whether we might have made a mistake in choosing our husbands or wives, God wants us to enjoy the gift of marriage and use it to His purposes.

I must tell you I feel great joy that God did not answer all of my prayers regarding "the right one" for me! The other day I saw a woman I had really liked when I was a teenager. At the time, I even thought she was "God's will" for me. But God said no. Back then, I groused about God's answer. But ah, the clarity of 20/20 hindsight! As I think of my wife today, all I can say is, "God knew what He was doing! His will is perfect!"

I have come across people who were not believers when they married; or if they were, they were not endeavoring to follow God's will in choosing a mate. Later on when times got rough, they were tempted toward divorce and they rationalized by saying, "I must have married the wrong person. God didn't bring us together, so it will probably be okay with Him if we divorce. Perhaps there is someone else God wants me to marry." I have even seen people go so far as to get involved in an affair with another Christian and justify it the same way: "God brought us together so He must want me to get divorced and marry this new person."

Friends, make no mistake—that is not the way it works. Even if you did not know the Lord when you got married, He knew you. He intends for you and your spouse to stay together and glorify Him in your marriage. One woman struggled to learn this lesson but finally came to understand that God intended her to stay married. She said, "I had a deep sense that it didn't matter why I married him, or that neither of us were Christians when we married. What we did for our own selfish desires, God meant for good. He will work it all out for the good of those who love him."

Those of us who are married have the privilege of living out God's perfect will for our married lives. His will for us, right now, is that we work hard to make our marriages the best they can be—even, as Romans 12:2 says, "good, pleasing and perfect."

PONDER

From the day you make that commitment [to say "I do"], your question about "the right person" is answered. He or she is the right person for you to stick to, love, cherish.

—TIM STAFFORD[20]

PROBE

- How does it alter your perspective to know that your marriage is definitely God's will for your life?
- Once you're confident that your marriage is God's will for you, how does that change your obligation to nurture this gift and make it all God intends it to be?

PRAY

Thank the Lord for the gracious gift of your marriage, and pray that He would guide you in making it "good, pleasing and perfect."

18

LOSING YOUR DESIRE

I have taken an oath and confirmed it,
that I will follow your righteous laws.
PSALM 119:106

This week is about commitment, and it's easy for me to define it, explain it, and exhort you to live by it. But what happens if you enter a season of marriage in which your commitment to *commitment* wanes? What happens if you lose your perspective, and even worse, lose your desire to fight for your marriage?

What happens if one day, you just don't want to be married anymore?

Our society does a good job of devaluing marriage and commitment and convincing people they have the right to follow their whims to happiness. More people are waking up one day and discovering they've completely lost the will to care about their vows anymore. The only way to go seems to be out the door.

Perhaps you'll never feel like this. But you may have found yourself in this position. You may be in it now, or you may experience it in the future. And if it ever happens to you, I want you to know how to deal with it.

First, remind yourself that you're dealing with feelings. They come and go, and they often don't tell us the truth. The truths of God's Word and His plan for your life don't change, regardless of your emotions about them. Acknowledge your feelings but don't give them more credit than they're due. In other words, don't take yourself so seriously.

Second, do the thing that you least want to do right now: spend more time with your spouse. It's especially important to enjoy leisure or fun activities together. You need to associate fun and good feelings with your spouse, so get into situations in which that can happen. You may be tempted to spend more time with other friends. Don't! Get out and have fun with your husband or wife.

Third, step up your efforts to actively love. Give compliments, leave notes, help around the house or yard, or arrange a special date. Give your spouse the opportunity to appreciate you, which will bring good feelings back. Don't wait for the *feelings* of love; just love by what you say and do. Scripture reminds us: "Dear children, let us stop just saying we love each other; let us really show it by our actions" (1 John 3:18 NLT).

Fourth, you are going to need to spend more time in prayer. God's will is *not* for you to be unhappy in your marriage, and He is always willing to step in and help. Pray for guidance, love, strength, courage. Allow God to be an active participant in your marriage. If you are too far gone for coherent words, just cry out (or whimper) to God, "Help!"

One woman had been struggling with the commitment aspect of her marriage and though she'd been married nine years, it came to the surface that she had never really come to grips with the "forever" part of the vow. She separated from her husband for a while, but she eventually made the decision to walk in pure obedience, regardless of her feelings. It was a true "dying to self" experience. She had to give up her right to act on her emotions. She handed it straight over to God and told Him she'd do what He asked.

Well, that woman was stunned by the blessings that came from her step of obedience and faith. God is restoring her marriage, and most astonishingly, He has restored her desire for the commitment. In fact, for the first time in her marriage, she is now able to say the word she had been avoiding without flinching. That word is "forever."

She has truly come to an understanding of "what God has joined together, let man not separate" (Matt.19:6).

Commitment is a decision, pure and simple. I've met so many people for whom that decision is a no-brainer. But I've met others who struggle with the "till death do us part" aspect of marriage. Sometimes you just have to clench your fists, close your eyes, and step out in complete faith and obedience, for no other reason than that God wants you to.

PONDER

Love is not a fluttering, dizzying emotion, gripping you one day, loosing you the next, but a rock-solid resolve to give yourself, day after day, to another.

—MARK BUCHANAN[21]

PROBE

- Think of times in which you knew your feelings were leading you away from truth. How did you handle it?
- Have you ever felt it must be God's will for you to be miserable? What caused you to feel this way, and how do you feel about it now?

PRAY

Ask God to build in you that rock-solid resolve you will need in order to give yourself to your spouse day after day.

19

THE MAGNITUDE OF VOWS

> *When a man makes a vow to the LORD or takes an*
> *oath to obligate himself by a pledge, he must not*
> *break his word but must do everything he said.*
>
> NUMBERS 30:2

"I, Greg, take you Catherine, to be my wife, to have and to hold from this day forward, for better or for worse, for richer, for poorer, in sickness and in health, to love and to cherish; from this day forward until death do us part."

We stand in the front of a church or on a grassy hill or a beach or in the judge's chambers, and we take a vow. We hear these words so often—recited by the young and old, the Christian and the atheist, the virgin and the divorcee, on television and in movies—that we seldom stop to think about the significance of taking a vow.

But God doesn't ever stop thinking about it. He takes our vows far more seriously than some of us do.

God places a huge premium on words. After all, what is His greatest gift to us besides Jesus Christ? His Word. By simply speaking, He brought the world into existence.

God's Word is sacred. And in His eyes, your word is sacred too. By your word, you bring a new entity into existence: your marriage.

We are reminded numerous times that when we give our word, we are expected to keep it. We are held accountable for every promise we've ever made (Matt. 5:37).

If you're not sure you can keep a pledge you make, you are better off not making it. Every vow we make is first, a promise to the Lord, and second, a promise to another person. You may have understood this at the time you got married; then again, maybe you didn't. But don't worry—it's never too late to make a recommitment, and this time, you make it to God first, then your spouse.

I read about a couple in Dallas who run a ministry devoted to spreading the message of hope for rebuilding damaged marriages. Their story is a miraculous one of restoration and healing, and its hallmark is that their new commitment—the commitment to "forever"—is one made first to God, and then to one another. This wasn't the case when they originally married. It happened only after much destruction and pain. But the new order of their vows is exactly what gives each of them their confidence in the marriage. They can look each other in the eye and say, "My commitment is first to God, and I will never betray Him by breaking my promise, therefore you can trust that my commitment to you is permanent."

Incidentally, this view of vows can help you in all areas of your marriage. Only make a promise if you fully intend to keep it. Don't say you'll wash the dishes if you're not going to do it. Only promise you'll pick up the dry cleaning if you mean it. The more you are consistent at upholding all the small pledges you make, the more your spouse will trust you and be confident in the security of your wedding vows.

"And whatever you do, whether in word or deed, do it all in the name of the Lord Jesus, giving thanks to God the Father through him" (Col. 3:17). There is no better way to look at your marital vows.

PONDER

What greater thing is there for two human souls, than to feel that they are joined for life—to strengthen each other in all labor, to rest on each other in all sorrow, to minister to each other in all pain, to be one with each other in silent unspeakable memories at the moment of the last parting?

—GEORGE ELIOT[22]

PROBE

- Why is the sacredness of your word so important to God?
- What are some ways you can use small daily promises and pledges to strengthen the overall vow of your marriage?

PRAY

Thank God for the amazing gift of His Word. Pray that you will always uphold your word, and that you will be immediately convicted if you don't.

20

REMEMBER THE COVENANT

*Whenever the rainbow appears in the clouds, I
will see it and remember the everlasting covenant
between God and all living creatures of every kind
on the earth.*

Genesis 9:16

God knew the importance of having a reminder of a promise. He's not the one who needs the reminder—we are. And so He set the rainbow in the clouds so that we would forevermore have a remembrance of His covenant with us, that "never again will all life be cut off by the waters of a flood" (Gen. 9:11).

What kind of reminders do you have of the commitment you made in marriage? I believe it's crucial to nurture your marriage on a daily basis and to have occasional concrete reminders of the vows you took.

Some people renew their vows when they've been married twenty-five or fifty years. This is a great reason for celebration! Some have chosen to repeat their vows on a regular basis, such as every year on their anniversary. And as you grow in your marriage relationship and in the Lord, your understanding of the vows will stretch and deepen year after year. You will be amazed at how profound your wedding vows really are!

Another idea is to have your actual wedding vows written up, framed, and hung in a place where you can see them. Then take the time to read them every once in a while and really think about their meaning. Ask yourself, *Am I upholding this vow every day, in every way possible?*

One couple was getting ready to celebrate their fiftieth wedding anniversary. They had planned an extravagant Caribbean cruise as a gift to themselves. Unfortunately, health problems intervened and the trip had to be cancelled at the last minute. What a heartbreak! They had been looking forward to the vacation, had intended to renew their vows, and had purchased new clothes for the voyage. But they decided that God must have had a better plan and were determined to make the best of it.

One month after their fiftieth, on the "month-iversary," they put on some of those new clothes, went out on a nice date, and renewed their vows. They had such a good time that they decided to do it more often. It's been two years since then, and this adorable couple has been celebrating and renewing their wedding covenant every single month. What a great remembrance of their commitment to one another!

Other people have their own ways of remembering their covenant. One woman said, "My husband and I mark the end of each day together by toasting. Whether it's fruit juice in crystal goblets in the summer, or herbal tea in ceramic mugs in winter, we snuggle up on the couch and relax in the last quiet moments of each day. I look forward all day long to our little ritual, and it is a gentle reminder that we're still a team, even when we've spent all day running in different directions."

Another offers, "Sometimes my husband will say, 'Will you marry me again today?' or I'll say, 'I think I'd like to marry you now.' We are acknowledging a moment of pleasure in our oneness. These little 'daily marryings' help solidify a truly good, long-term marriage."

Anything you can do to help yourself remember your commitment will be a blessing for your marriage. In the same way that some people memorize Scripture as a way of "hiding God's Word in their hearts," why not memorize your wedding vows? You will benefit from whispering to yourself in tough times, "For better, for worse," or in times of financial hardship, "For richer, for poorer." Your own vows may have been unique and more complex, but whatever they were, it helps to be reminded of them because you will be held accountable for them!

God placed a rainbow in the sky to remind us of His covenant. What kind of rainbow can you hang to remind you of yours?

PONDER

If you don't make a total commitment to whatever you're doing, then you start looking to bail out the first time the boat starts leaking. It's tough enough getting that boat to shore with everybody rowing, let alone when a guy stands up and starts putting his life jacket on.

—LOU HOLTZ[23]

PROBE

- Why is it so important to have a tangible reminder of a promise you have made?
- Make a list of ways you and your spouse could begin to incorporate reminders of your vows into your regular daily lives.

PRAY

Ask that God will never let you forget the significance of your marital vows, and that He will increase your comprehension of their meaning.

13

THE VIRTUE OF SELFLESSNESS

This week we will be looking at selflessness as a discipline and a virtue. Our innate self-centeredness is one of the major struggles of the Christian life. Our goal is to be centered on Christ and to think of others before ourselves, but we constantly battle our self-focus in order to achieve this. As you work through these five days, think of ways you can put your marriage and the needs of your mate above your own.

21

OUR "ME FIRST" SOCIETY

> *But mark this: There will be terrible times in the*
> *last days. People will be lovers of themselves, lovers*
> *of money, boastful . . . lovers of pleasure rather*
> *than lovers of God—having a form of godliness*
> *but denying its power.*
>
> 2 TIMOTHY 3:1–2, 4–5

It is hammered into our minds through every form of media. We see it in the magazines, television programs, and movies. We hear it in the music. What is that message?

Seek your own happiness.

Whatever the cost—it doesn't matter. We deserve happiness. It's our *right*. We are essentially told to believe, *Everything revolves around me. I am the only thing that matters.*

Me first.

In fact, the Bible tells us it would be paramount in the last days, a time in which I believe we are now living: Paul told Timothy that people will be "lovers of themselves" and "lovers of pleasure rather than lovers of God."

Look out for number one, we're told, because if you don't, nobody else will. It's a dog-eat-dog world. Let the others fend for themselves. Or, as Humphrey Bogart said in *Casablanca*, "I stick my neck out for nobody."

We've been brainwashed to believe that self-esteem is the holy grail to make our lives work. You might be thinking, *Wait a second. I thought that all of the problems of our culture could be traced to low self-esteem.* Yet it is because of our self-love, our obsession with self, that we have many of the problems in our culture today. In our entertainment-saturated society, we are living in an altered state of reality. We live with illusions of what life should be: the fantasy of the perfect romantic and sexual relationship, the fantasy of the perfect husband or the perfect wife, the fantasy of the perfect lifestyle. Yet these are nonexistent things we chase after.

Our culture is busy telling us "Every man for himself," but is anybody stopping to remember what the Bible says? Galatians 6:2 tells us precisely the opposite: "Carry each other's burdens, and in this way you will fulfill the law of Christ." We are called to go against the cultural tide of self-centeredness, to live Christ-centered and others-centered lives.

Selfishness is at the base of human nature. We have been fighting it since man has been on earth. A blatant example comes in Genesis 4:9, where we have an older brother shamelessly declaring his self-centeredness and utter lack of care for another: "Then the LORD said to Cain, 'Where is your brother Abel?' 'I don't know,' he replied. 'Am I my brother's keeper?'"

Cain was hiding a hideous murder he'd committed, but he wasn't bothering to hide his callous self-interest. That's similar to the situation we have in our culture today. People are not in the least bit ashamed of their self-focus; in fact, they are proud of it!

The belief that the individual is supreme has devastating ramifications for society. We now have the "individual's right to choose" (choose murder, that is). People campaign for gay marriage because "it's all about the individual's right to happiness." Every immoral lifestyle is justified on the basis of "personal choice."

Friends, this is the environment in which we are endeavoring to live out healthy, principled, God-honoring lives. I think it's crucial to look around us, see what we're up against, and brace ourselves for the battle. Let's spend this week looking at ways to become selfless in regards to our marriages.

PONDER

We live in an age in which people will not commit themselves to something unless they believe they will get something out of it—some kind of benefit or privilege. "What's in it for me?" is the question often heard. . . . This mind-set has unfortunately found its way into the Christian church. People want to know what they will get out of Christianity if they commit themselves to it. How will Christ enrich my life, make me feel better, or deal with my problems?

—Bill Muehlenberg[24]

PROBE

- In what ways do you personally struggle with self-centeredness?
- How has self-focus impacted your marriage in the past?

PRAY

Ask God to search your heart and gently reveal your own selfishness, along with the strength and resources to overcome it.

22

PUTTING MARRIAGE FIRST

Live a life worthy of the calling you have received.
Be completely humble and gentle; be patient,
bearing with one another in love.

Ephesians 4:1–2

Concepts such as sacrifice, selflessness, and keeping one's commitment are rarely discussed today, so we carry the same me-first mentality into our marriages. We get married believing our beloveds are the ones to make us happy. We have an expectation that our spouses will fulfill us and meet our needs. When it seems they are no longer doing this, we feel we have the right to cut our losses and move on. They might not come right out and verbalize it, but it is the way many people feel in their hearts.

We all have occasional (or frequent) difficulties in our marriages, but the problem is rarely what it seems. It's not money or careers or children or in-laws per se, though they can certainly all contribute. The problem with most marriages today could be summed up in one word: self. James asks, "What causes fights and quarrels among you? Don't they come from your desires that battle within you?" (James 4:1). If I have conflict in my marriage over finances, it's probably because of the greed and need for control that I brought into the relationship. If my marriage suffers because of career concerns, it's most likely due to pride or ambition that clouds my vision and makes me put my career over my family.

We bring these problems into our marriages because of our sinful inclination toward ourselves, which often leads to such inane sayings as: "I am no longer happy in my marriage." "I need my own space." "My mate is no longer meeting my needs." "I am going to go find myself." This thinking sounds reasonable to many people, because it is what our culture teaches.

We live in a society that is, in many ways, openly hostile to the family itself. Activists do everything in their power to undermine and redefine what marriage and family really are. Unfortunately the culture's values are so powerful and pervading that they can easily eclipse the teachings people hear in church once a week. That is what destroys so many marriages. When life doesn't measure up to what we think it should, we simply say, "I must go and search for it somewhere else."

Understand what I am saying here. I am not suggesting that you cannot be happy and fulfilled in a marriage, and in fact, I think this topic is so important that I'm going to discuss it further on Day 35. What I am saying is that if you go into marriage with the expectation of your spouse's meeting all your needs, and without any real concern about your meeting his or hers, you will be disappointed. If you hold in your heart the motive of marrying someone so you can bring happiness to his or her life, and so you can meet your spouse's needs and bring him or her fulfillment, you have a much better chance of a good marriage.

Think about it: you cannot control anyone but yourself, and even that is an iffy proposition much of the time. If the happiness of your marriage is based on what someone else does, you're doomed. But if you allow your marital happiness to flow from what you are doing for your spouse, from how well you are nurturing and supporting your marriage, then you have a greater likelihood of success. It's logical that putting the marriage first, not yourself, creates a greater opportunity for marital happiness.

While it is true that selfishness is part of human nature, it is not true that we're beyond the hope of changing. The Bible tells us, "If anyone is in Christ, he is a new creation; old things have passed away; behold, all things have become new" (2 Cor. 5:17 NKJV). God is telling us that we have a new nature, and we are to live by new standards. And He has given us new power with which to do it. Let's take hold of His power and begin asking ourselves every single day, *Am I putting myself—or my marriage—first?*

PONDER

All of these attitudes—envy, jealousy, bitterness, an unforgiving and retaliatory spirit, and a critical and gossiping spirit—defile us and keep us from being holy before God. . . . We cloak these defiling thoughts under the guise of justice and righteous indignation. But we need to pray daily for humility and honesty to see these sinful attitudes for what they really are, and then for grace and discipline to root them out of our minds and replace them with thoughts pleasing to God.

—JERRY BRIDGES[25]

PROBE

- What are some of the issues that have caused conflict in your marriage, and how can you trace them back to problems with yourself? (No fair looking at the problems of your spouse!)
- List some ways you can begin to take the focus off yourself and instead put your attention on Christ, your spouse, and your family.

PRAY

Pray that you will be able to distinguish between being self-focused and being centered on Christ.

23

YOU'VE LOST THAT LOVIN' FEELING

*And if anyone gives even a cup of cold water to
one of these little ones because he is my disciple,
I tell you the truth, he will certainly not lose his
reward.*

MATTHEW 10:42

God has called us, His children, to a higher standard, a new way of thinking and behaving. As Christians, we cannot think as this world thinks or act as it acts. God says, "Come out from them and be separate" (2 Cor. 6:17). In Romans 12:2 we read, "Do not conform any longer to the pattern of this world, but be transformed by the renewing of your mind."

So, selfishness must be abandoned, and in its place, we must find a new, selfless, God-honoring life in which we put what God's Word says above our own desires. The Bible tells us to esteem others better than ourselves. If every married couple did this one thing, our homes would be transformed overnight. If you put the needs of your spouse above your own, and thought of your spouse's happiness and their fulfillment above yours, it would radically change your home.

Dr. Laura Schlessinger says,

The notion of love as a gift, as a verb, as an attitude, as a commitment, is a revelation to some. Unfortunately, love is usually looked at as a feeling that comes over you and makes you happy; and of course, *if* you're happy, *then* you behave nicely. Somehow, the notion is out there that you're entitled to behave badly if you don't feel that lovin' feeling. . . . This sense of entitlement comes from a culture that has elevated feelings over obligation, responsibility, and commitment.[26]

We need to look at love as an action word—and take action whether we feel like it or not. There are hundreds of small and large acts of selflessness you can do on a regular basis to keep your marriage humming. One of the most wonderful gifts you can offer is to pray with—and pray over—your loved one. In the words of one happy wife, "My husband prays so tenderly over me when I'm hurting. And in church, every Sunday before we take Communion, he pulls me to him and prays over us together, and then he serves me the Communion. This never fails to bring a tear to my eye. I cannot imagine feeling more loved." This act of love doesn't take much effort on the part of her husband, but you can see what wonderful rewards this couple is reaping.

Another husband says, "I used to sit back and enjoy the way my wife took care of me: bringing me coffee in the morning, preparing my favorite meals, and arranging fun trips that I would enjoy. It wasn't until she almost left the marriage that I finally realized I needed to take care of her too. I had to learn to put her desires ahead of mine, which, sad to say, didn't come naturally. Now I do things I never would have thought of before, like making her favorite salad for dinner and taking her to a nice hotel rather than on a camping trip. I finally learned that it's not always about me."

Aha! Now we're talking.

We can put our spouses first in the smallest of ways: letting them sleep while we get the kids ready for school, filling their cars with gas, packing them a lunch to bring to work, setting aside time to spend alone with them each day. We can also express our love for them through more significant acts of selflessness. Unfortunately, there are times in life when our spouses are ill or injured and need us to give up almost everything in order to care for them. If we have been practic-

ing daily acts of selflessness, we will be ready for these times and able to approach them generously and graciously.

PONDER

Love, you know, seeks to make happy rather than to be happy.

—Ralph Connor[27]

PROBE

- Why is it so hard sometimes to act lovingly when we are not feeling it? How can we get ourselves to behave in a way that opposes our feelings?
- Make a list of ways you can put your own desires aside and serve your mate instead.

PRAY

Ask God for the discipline to put down your own desires more often in favor of the desires or needs of your marriage.

24

DYING TO SELF

*Do nothing out of selfish ambition or vain
conceit, but in humility consider others better than
yourselves. Each of you should look not only to your
own interests, but also to the interests of others.*
PHILIPPIANS 2:3–4

Our society has developed a warped view of self-sacrifice. We are concerned with "losing ourselves" and afraid of giving too much. I think this is due to the fact that many people give of themselves for the wrong reasons, and with unspiritual motives, without even realizing it. So they burn out and feel used up and unloved. How does this happen?

It is increasingly common for people to walk away from a marriage because they feel as they give, give, give, and never get anything in return. This is often a legitimate grievance and needs to be addressed in the marriage. At the same time, if you feel this way, I recommend you examine your motives for all this "giving." Are you truly giving "as to the Lord"? It's possible you may, instead, be giving for any number of basically selfish reasons:

- It helps you maintain your self-image as the "perfect" one in the relationship.
- It keeps your spouse feeling indebted to you.
- It makes it difficult for your spouse to ever be angry with you for anything.

These are just a few possible ways you may be "self-sacrificing" with impure motives. Jesus said, "If anyone would come after me, he must deny himself and take up his cross and follow me" (Matt. 16:24). Notice that denying yourself is for the purpose of *following Him*, not for any other emotional or psychological reason. If you're giving of yourself without being constantly filled by the Spirit, you will soon be empty.

When you give love to another in the form of selfless actions, you should not be looking for earthly rewards but heavenly ones. Jesus said, "Do not store up for yourselves treasures on earth, where moth and rust destroy, and where thieves break in and steal. But store up for yourselves treasures in heaven, where moth and rust do not destroy, and where thieves do not break in and steal" (Matt. 6:19–20). If you are putting your own desires behind those of your mate, approach it as if you were doing it for the Lord Himself. Dedicate your service to Him, and let your heart be satisfied that your heavenly storehouse is being filled.

A life of faith is full of paradoxes, and here's one: if you are sacrificing yourself for another and doing it as for the Lord, you will not lose yourself but will actually come closer to finding self. By that I mean you will begin to become the person God made you to be. At the same time, you will care far less about yourself and you will not worry so much about your personal desires—having allowed your "self" to take a backseat to other people and to Christ.

Marriage is one of the greatest gifts God has given to help us become "transformed into his likeness with ever-increasing glory" (2 Cor. 3:18). It is in this arena that we can practice—day after day, year after year—dying to ourselves. It is meant to be a safe and loving environment in which we can strive to serve, to give of ourselves, to follow Him and yet be able to make mistakes and be forgiven.

As you continue thinking about ways to exemplify selflessness in your marriage, take comfort in knowing that God sees every little act of service, every feat of self-denial, and records it in heaven. Hopefully your spouse will be so awed by your devotion that he or she can't help but be just as loving toward you. But regardless of how your mate responds, be filled with joy in the knowledge that you are serving your Savior.

PONDER

The one thing we can never get enough of is love. And the one thing we can never give enough of is love.

—Henry Miller[28]

PROBE

- If you feel you've been a giver in your marriage, take some time to prayerfully examine your motives. How spiritual as opposed to selfish have they been?
- What is most difficult for you to accept about the concept of storing up treasures in heaven?

PRAY

Ask the Lord to continue to transform you into His image by helping you be as selfless as possible in your marriage with the right motives.

25

HAPPY OR HOLY?

*If a man has recently married, he must not be sent
to war or have any other duty laid on him. For
one year he is to be free to stay at home and bring
happiness to the wife he has married.*

DEUTERONOMY 24:5

$\mathcal{A}$ll this talk of selflessness in marriage might be making you
feel a bit hopeless. Right about now you may be asking, "Isn't there a
place for happiness in marriage too?"

The simple answer is yes! God did intend for happiness to have
a place in marriage. You see in Deuteronomy 24:5 that God allowed
newly married men to stay home from war an entire year for the express purpose of bringing happiness to their wives. That's not am-
biguous—it's pretty clear what God was saying here!

However, God's definition of happiness is usually a little different from ours. We tend to think of happiness as an emotion that
comes and goes depending on circumstances. God is referring to *joy*,
a deeper, more lasting feeling of well-being that persists in spite of
changing circumstances. True joy comes from a vital relationship
with Christ.

If you are pursuing Christ and endeavoring to replace "me first"
with a selfless attitude in marriage, then you are pursuing holiness.
Clearly, the Lord wants us to do this. The Bible says, "Try to live in
peace with everyone, and seek to live a clean and holy life, for those

who are not holy will not see the Lord" (Heb. 12:14 NLT). But what does it mean to be holy?

Perhaps if we spelled the word differently, it would help. Try this: *wholly*.

In other words, if you want to be a holy person, seek to wholly follow the Lord. That was the secret of a man named Caleb who was very close to God. Caleb said, "I wholly followed the LORD my God" (Josh. 14:8 NKJV).

But the question arises: if your heart is full of joy, will you be happy all the time? Undoubtedly the answer is no. You could experience all kinds of trials that preclude circumstantial happiness yet still have the joy that comes directly from Christ.

Jesus said, "I have told you this so that my joy may be in you and that your joy may be complete" (John 15:11). When His joy is in us, our joy is *complete*—meaning we don't need anything else in order to be joyful. His love is enough. *The Life Application Study Bible* tells us, "True joy transcends the rolling waves of circumstance. Joy comes from a consistent relationship with Jesus Christ. When our lives are intertwined with his, he will help us walk through adversity without sinking into debilitating lows, and manage prosperity without moving into deceptive highs."[29]

So, looking back at Deuteronomy 24:5, what do you think the newly married man was supposed to do in that first year? He was supposed to tend to his wife unselfishly, build the marriage relationship, and simultaneously develop his relationship with God through his holy, selfless service. This seems to me God's perfect recipe for joy in marriage.

I am troubled that some people might be making a dichotomy out of happy versus holy because they are unhappy in their marriages. They are looking for hope, something that would give them a reason to stay in a marriage they perceive as personally unfulfilling. They're thinking that if they can't be happy, then maybe they can at least be holy. I am suggesting that if you seek to be holy you will, in time, find happiness as well—not from seeking it but from seeking the Lord.

You can also find contentment. When the apostle Paul said,

"I have learned to be content whatever the circumstances" (Phil. 4:11), he truly meant *content*. He didn't mean some sort of resigned, gritting-your-teeth and sticking-it-out determination. He was referring to a deep-down feeling of peace and joy. This is what God wants for you in marriage. I hope that this week's focus on selfless service in marriage helps you to find contentment, as you accept God's will for your life and marriage. This contentment does not come from what we have but from whom we know. The Scripture reminds us, "Be content with what you have, because God has said, 'Never will I leave you; never will I forsake you'" (Heb. 13:5).

The Lord is there with you each step of the way, willing to help you be the spouse He has called you to be.

PONDER

Happiness and self-fulfillment [are] natural by-products of marriage as God intended it, but not the primary purpose for marriage. The first marriage [Adam and Eve] was at least as much about relating to God as it was about relating to each other.

—AL JANSSEN[30]

PROBE

- Think of times in which you may have felt unhappy with your spouse. Did you still feel the deep-down joy of Christ, or do you sometimes find it elusive?
- How can we develop our relationships with God and with our spouses so that we, like Paul, learn to be content whatever the circumstances?

PRAY

Ask God to show you how to pursue Him instead of fickle happiness and to grant you the joy of truly knowing Him.

13

SUBMISSION AND HEADSHIP

This week the subject is submission—not a popular one these days! Read this section with the knowledge that this topic applies to both husbands and wives, who must submit to Christ and to one another. Yet God asks a special type of submission from wives, and this is sometimes misunderstood. Take the time to contemplate and discuss this topic until you are comfortable with your understanding.

26

GRACIOUS OBEDIENCE

I want you to know that the head of every man is Christ, the head of woman is man, and the head of Christ is God.

1 CORINTHIANS 11:3 (NKJV)

No difference exists between men and women in their basic standing before God. Still, we cannot afford to miss an important principle of family authority expressed in the New Testament. The apostle Paul explained that man is the head of woman and Christ is the head of man, just as God is the head of Christ.

Before anyone objects to Paul's teaching, let's first try to understand his statement: "The head of Christ is God." What exactly did he mean?

The Bible reveals to us a holy Trinity: the Father, the Son, and the Holy Spirit. These three persons constitute not three gods, but one God. Each member of the Trinity is fully God. The Son is just as much God as is the Father, and the Holy Spirit is just as much God as is the Son. Together they comprise the single, triune God.

Nevertheless, although these persons remain eternally coequal, the Bible teaches that God the Father is the head of God the Son—not in essence or in nature, but in role or function.

Jesus—whom Isaiah called "Mighty God" (Isa. 9:6)—laid aside many of the privileges of deity and took upon Himself the form of a servant, becoming "obedient to death—even death on a cross" (Phil.

2:8). When Jesus walked this earth, He repeatedly demonstrated His subservience to His Father. He spoke the words of the Father. He submitted to the wishes of the Father. Though He was "in very nature God" (Phil. 2:6), though "God was pleased to have all his fullness dwell in him" (Col. 1:19), and though Jesus is "the radiance of God's glory and the exact representation of his being" (Heb. 1:3), He willingly placed Himself in an obedient position.

In the same way, though the husband and the wife remain equal in their standing before God, in order for the family to function harmoniously, the woman—with no loss of dignity—is to willingly submit to the headship of her husband. Now, let's not misunderstand the word *submit*. It doesn't mean that you are a slave or a doormat. It simply means to put another's rights and desires ahead of your own. Just as the husband is to always look to God for leadership, putting God's desires ahead of his own, so the wife is to look to her husband. This is easy if a wife knows her husband is listening to God!

Just prior to his exhortation for wives to submit to husbands, Paul calls all Christians to submit to one another. We spent the last week discussing this concept—selflessness in marriage and in life. Although God calls for a leadership hierarchy, He also calls husbands to be completely submitted to Him, and for husbands and wives to "submit to one another" (Eph. 5:21). Wives are to willingly follow their husbands' leadership, and husbands are to set aside their own interests to care for their wives.

To quote a statement of faith published by the Southern Baptist Convention:

> The husband and wife are of equal worth before God, since both are created in God's image. The marriage relationship models the way God relates to His people. A husband is to love his wife as Christ loved the church. He has the God-given responsibility to provide for, to protect, and to lead his family. A wife is to submit graciously to the servant leadership of her husband even as the church willingly submits to the headship of Christ.[31]

Well said—and you know what else? It works! God intends that a husband's submission to Him will make it easy for the wife to cheerfully respect, help, and cooperate with her husband. In marriages where both husband and wife have a strong relationship with the Lord and they both try to put each other's needs first, submission is not an issue. Their love grows as together they submit to one another and to the Lord Jesus Christ.

PONDER

Note that Ephesians 5:22 explains that when you submit to your husband, you're really submitting to the Lord. One friend said that what helps her to submit is to imagine that Jesus is standing right behind her husband. She imagines herself looking right at Jesus as she tells her husband she'll follow his request.

—Melanie Chitwood[32]

PROBE

- Discuss or journal your own thoughts about submission in marriage. How do you feel about it?
- How might the concept of submission be misunderstood and misused by both husband and wife?

PRAY

Ask the Lord to show you how to be constantly submitted to Him and to your spouse.

27

A WOMAN'S WISDOM

David said to Abigail, "Praise be to the Lord, the
God of Israel, who has sent you today to meet me.
May you be blessed for your good judgment and
for keeping me from bloodshed this day and from
avenging myself with my own hands."

1 SAMUEL 25:32–33

As the head of my home, I am a man in authority. As a follower of Christ, I am also a man under authority. As such, I have a spiritual responsibility to make the best decisions possible for my home, which means getting the best counsel I can—and that, more often than not, comes from my wife.

I think any man who understands godly leadership will greatly value what his wife has to say. God has placed me in authority as the head of my home, but that doesn't mean I stand around barking orders to Cathe. I recognize that she is an equal partner in this marriage, and therefore I seek her input. I urgently want to know her opinion.

I can think of multiple situations in which I have been following a certain course, but after I've talked with my wife and heard her point of view, I will think, *Hmmm. I don't think I should go this way after all.*

I do not find it necessary in most cases to say, "Look, wife—I am the man! I am God's appointed leader, so we will go with my decision!" The majority of the time, Cathe and I will work out a solution and move forward together, and any husband who knows anything about life will do the same. I know David was glad that he listened to the counsel of Abigail—and that was before they were married!

We find the story in 1 Samuel 25. When a stubborn and surly man named Nabal (even his name means "foolish") deeply offended David and his men, David determined to wipe out the man's household. When Abigail, Nabal's intelligent and beautiful wife, discovered what her arrogant husband had done, she sought out David with gifts and persuaded him to avoid revenge.

David, astonished by the woman's wisdom, exclaimed, "May you be blessed for your good judgment and for keeping me from bloodshed this day." Later, when Nabal died, David himself married the man's remarkable widow.

Now, what would have happened had David ignored the advice of this most capable woman? For one thing, biblical history might well have been a great deal poorer. If David had carried out his rash act, he might have disqualified himself from the lofty position God intended for him.

Not every wife is an Abigail. But most women, if they are confident in their husbands' love and respect for them, will be able to speak up when they believe they have wisdom from which their husbands can benefit. Of course, some women tend to come on a little too strongly, unfortunately leading their husbands to disregard or stop listening to whatever they have to say. I advise all women to pray and study and do their best to adjust their interactions to show respect and love for their husbands, so that their marriages would have the chance to benefit from their wisdom.

I also know there are too many Nabals who don't appreciate the wisdom and insight that God has imparted to their wives. God has given you your wife as a gift, knowing she is exactly what you need. She not only knows you, she has a unique intelligence and perspective intended to be a complement to you. Wise husbands let their Abigails shine!

PONDER

A man who fears the Lord not only expects His Savior to hear and act on his cries for help, but he also follows His Savior's example.

He, too, is attentive to the cries of his loved ones. He listens to them because God listens to him. A Christ-like man strives to become like the Master, who was a master listener.

—Floyd McClung Jr.[33]

PROBE

- Why do you think God established a leadership hierarchy in the family, even while reminding men and women of their equal status before Him?
- Consider how you and your spouse manage the balance of leadership and submission in your home. How well are you doing? Could anything be improved?

PRAY

Wives, ask God to show you the perspective He wants you to impart to your husbands and to give you a pleasing and humble spirit in which to relay it. Husbands, pray for the wisdom and humility to hear and receive your wives' counsel.

28

TAMING THE CURSE

Submit to one another out of reverence for Christ.
EPHESIANS 5:21

$\mathcal{S}$omething significant resulted from Adam and Eve's sin besides death entering the human race. This part of the curse affects our marriages to this day: after Eve sinned in the garden, the Lord had something very important to say to her: "Your desire will be for your husband, and he will rule over you" (Gen. 3:16).

It is important to keep in mind that this verse was part of the curse. Looking at the words in the original language will help us understand a dynamic that is a cause of the tension between men and women to this very day.

The word that is translated "desire" is the same Hebrew term used in Genesis 4; it comes from a root word that means "to compel, to impel, to urge, or to seek control over." In Genesis 4:7, the Lord warned Cain, "Sin is crouching at your door; it *desires* to have you, but you must master it" (emphasis mine). God was essentially saying, "Cain, sin wants to control you, but you must control sin."

In light of this close contextual meaning of the word "desire," the curse on Eve was that woman's desire would be to assume the place of her husband's headship. She would want to rule her husband.

With Adam and Eve's sin and the curse that followed came the distortion of the ideas of submissiveness and authority. In other words, woman has a sinful inclination to usurp the authority of her husband. In the same way, man has a sinful inclination to put his wife under his feet and disregard his own submission to God. Both are equally wrong.

"Your desire will be for your husband": God says wives will want to control their husbands, and most women will agree they have this instinct. Many women say, "I'm just a control freak!" Yes, you are. It was part of the curse of sin.

"And he will rule over you": here's the other half of the equation. Men are naturally dominant. They have this instinct to not allow their wives—or anyone, for that matter—to control them. Obviously this need to rule over their wives comes in direct opposition to the wives' controlling nature. A curse, indeed! But the Bible gives us clear instructions on how to live together without constant conflict.

Ephesians 5:21 tells us that all Christians are to "submit to one another out of reverence for Christ." This is the only way to live in harmony despite the curse. We need to treat each other as we would treat the Lord Himself, with love, respect, and deference. But we already know that we have a bent towards selfishness and sinful domination of each other. How are we to overcome this?

God says, "Be filled with the Spirit" (Eph. 5:18). You see, we can't do this in our own strength. A husband cannot love and lead his wife in a Christlike way, and a wife cannot lovingly submit to her husband, without the help of the Holy Spirit. You need God's help. If you are filled with the Spirit, you will have the power to obey these commands.

God even tells us how we can stay filled with the Spirit. Ephesians 5:19–20 says, "Speak to one another with psalms, hymns and spiritual songs. Sing and make music in your heart to the Lord, always giving thanks to God the Father for everything, in the name of our Lord Jesus Christ." In other words, fill your heart and mind with the Word of God, sing praises to Him constantly, and be grateful for your blessings.

Don't you think if we all lived this way, our marriages would be filled with harmony and the awesome love of Christ? How wonderful that God gives us commands only with the power to fulfill them! Husband, wife, be filled with the Spirit, submit to one another, and see your marriage flourish.

PONDER

There is nothing more lovely in life than the union of two people whose love for one another has grown through the years from the small acorn of passion to a great rooted tree. Surviving all vicissitudes, and rich with its manifold branches, every leaf holding its own significance.

—VITA SACKVILLE-WEST[34]

PROBE

- In your marriage, how have the wife's need for control and the husband's need for dominance asserted themselves?
- What are some ways the two of you submit to one another out of reverence for Christ?

PRAY

Ask the Lord to help you both stay filled with the Spirit so that you may submit to one another and to Him.

29

WHY AND HOW

Wives, submit to your husbands as to the Lord.
EPHESIANS 5:22

The apostle Paul did not instruct wives merely to submit to their husbands and leave it at that; he also told them how, and he told them why. He gave them a motive and a manner of submitting.

The motive of submission is obedience to God, and the manner of submission is "as to the Lord." Wives are to submit to their husbands as if they were doing so to the Lord Himself. God instructs wives to submit to their husbands as an act of submission to Christ.

Colossians 3:23 echoes the same idea: "Whatever you do, work at it with all your heart, as working for the Lord, not for men." This passage doesn't apply specifically to a wife submitting to her husband; it applies to all of us. We are all to submit to those in authority over us, whether to employers, teachers, law enforcement personnel, or others. "Everyone must submit himself to the governing authorities, for there is no authority except that which God has established. The authorities that exist have been established by God," Paul wrote in Romans 13:1. "Give everyone what you owe him: If you owe taxes, pay taxes; if revenue, then revenue; if respect, then respect; if honor, then honor" (v. 7).

We may not always appreciate what someone in authority asks us to do, but we should respond according to the following principle: *What would I do if it were Jesus asking me to do this?*

Your boss might say, "I want you to go and move those boxes." You might immediately think, *Get somebody else to move those boxes. I don't want to. Besides, I am on a break.* But if you put Jesus into the equation, then you will move those boxes; in fact, you will get to work both quickly and happily. Why? Because as a Christian, you take joy in doing whatever the Lord commands you.

Wives, let's say you receive a knock at your door. You look to see who it is, and you find Jesus standing there, so you open the door to let Him in. Would you then say, "Jesus, I'm kind of busy. Why don't You go into the kitchen and get Yourself a snack? I'll be with You in a moment." Of course not. I'm sure you would say, "Lord, please come in, sit down, make Yourself at home! Are You hungry? Why don't I get You a snack? In fact, it would be my privilege to make You a fabulous home-cooked meal! Let me get Rachael Ray on the phone."

Now, I am not saying that every time your husband's stomach rumbles you need to whip out the pots and pans and prepare a banquet. I am speaking about an attitude, one that desires to serve and to please, not out of flattery or fear, but out of love. We all can benefit from cultivating this attitude, both in our marriages and in our lives in general.

Husbands, it would be tempting to take advantage of being treated like a king, taking for granted your wives' loving care. You could easily abuse the situation, becoming demanding and expecting them to cater to your every whim. You might begin to forget that when they take care of you, they are often setting aside their own needs or desires for a time. Remember your own call to love your wife sacrificially, "as Christ loved the church." She is asked to submit to you as to the Lord, and you are also asked to emulate the Lord. So love her, and do not mistreat her!

The key is, you want to do your very best for Him. Why? Because He is Jesus and you love Him. This is what God is saying to both husbands and wives. Submit to your husband as to the Lord. Do it as an act of worship to Jesus Christ. That changes things, doesn't it?

PONDER

In obeying her husband, the Christian wife is obeying the Lord who has sanctioned the marriage contract. It should be noted that all Paul says is within the context of a Christian marriage. He is not implying that women are inferior to men or that all women should be subject to men. The subjection, moreover, is voluntary, not coerced. The Christian wife who promises to obey does so because her vow is "to the Lord."

—A. Skevington Wood[35]

PROBE

- How does it change your attitude if you are committed to doing something not for its own sake but "as for the Lord"?
- Why is it so difficult for people in our society today to understand and accept the concept of submission?

PRAY

Ask God to help you submit to Him in full obedience, and to teach you to do things "as for the Lord."

30

THE LIMITS TO SUBMISSION

Wives, submit to your husbands, as is fitting in the Lord.

COLOSSIANS 3:18

If wives are to submit to their husbands "as is fitting in the Lord," does that mean they are to obey all demands, even those that violate their consciences or the Word of God?

No, it doesn't. If a husband were to ask his wife to do something unscriptural, God calls the wife to respectfully decline. As Peter and the other apostles replied to those who demanded that they stop preaching in the name of Jesus, "We must obey God rather than men!" (Acts 5:29).

But let's get practical. Clearly, if your husband asks you to do something immoral or unethical, you should feel under no biblical constraint to agree, because the request violates Scripture. Yet sometimes your husband may have a request that is not a violation of Scripture yet goes against your own judgment. Perhaps it is a question of child rearing, or vacation planning, or sound financial management. What should you say?

I don't think there's anything wrong with reminding your husband of the great responsibility of leadership. Your husband may say, "I want to buy a new [fill in the blank]." You could respond, "Dear, you know that we are really not in a position to do that this month. I have been looking over our finances. We just don't have the resources. Maybe we should wait a little while?"

"No," he may argue. "We are going to do it now." If he refuses to budge, you can wash your hands of the matter by saying, "Okay, dear. If you believe the Lord is leading you to do this as the head of this home, we are with you."

Don't be surprised if he later says (after storming out and slamming a couple of doors), "I changed my mind."

There is nothing wrong with a wife offering her input and telling her husband what she thinks—and any reasonable husband will welcome it. Yet suppose your husband wants you to do something clearly wrong, and you tell him you cannot because it goes against Scripture. He replies, "I want you to go along with me. After all, your Bible says you are supposed to submit to your husband!"

"Yes," you could then reply, "but it also adds the phrase 'as is fitting in the Lord'—and this just isn't fitting. You are asking me to do something that dishonors God, and I cannot do that." Always remember that God never asks a Christian wife to violate, in the name of submission, what His Word clearly teaches. Nor would He ask you to stand around and be a punching bag for some abusive man.

I am not advocating any heavy-handed "holier than thou" attitude in which you berate your husband for not being a good Christian like you. In fact, that's the worst thing you could do. The best way to handle this, wives, is tenderly and with love. Believe me: men get their feathers ruffled if they feel they are being scolded! As his wife, you know how to talk to your husband sweetly to get his attention. That's the spirit and the tone of voice you should use if you need to deny your husband's wishes.

Just keep in mind, wives, that God will never ask you to submit if that means violating what the Bible teaches. In that case, you can refuse with a clear conscience. And husbands, don't try to take advantage of your leadership position. This will always come back to bite you. There are no limits in our submission to the Lord, but submission to one another is a different matter. True love for one another will make those limits clear.

PONDER

The husband does not replace Christ as the woman's supreme authority. She must never follow her husband's leadership into sin. But even where a Christian wife may have to stand with Christ against the sinful will of her husband, she can still have a spirit of submission. She can show by her attitude and behavior that she does not like resisting his will and that she longs for him to forsake sin and lead in righteousness so that her disposition to honor him as head can again produce harmony.

—John Piper[36]

PROBE

- Have you ever been in a situation in which you were asked to do something you felt violated biblical commands? What did you do?
- How are we to exhibit a spirit of submission if we really don't have one? Is there any advantage in faking it?

PRAY

Pray that neither of you will be tempted to lead the other down a sinful path in the name of submission or anything else.

THESE IMMORAL TIMES

This is not an easy subject to address, especially if you are doing this devotional with your spouse. I want you to know that whether you have a strong, healthy marriage that has never been touched by this type of sin, or whether you and your spouse have struggled with some level of immorality or infidelity, it is important to work through this section. Be as honest as you can with yourself, with God, and with your spouse when it comes to these issues. This is as real as it gets.

31

A STEALTH ATTACK

They have become filled with every kind of wickedness, evil, greed and depravity. They are full of envy, murder, strife, deceit and malice. They are gossips, slanderers, God-haters, insolent, arrogant and boastful; they invent ways of doing evil; they disobey their parents; they are senseless, faithless, heartless, ruthless.

ROMANS 1:29–31

𝓘t seems as though everywhere you look, marriages are falling apart. So little is out there to strengthen and support the family. These are the perilous days warned of in the Bible (see 2 Tim. 3:1–9). These are the times of wickedness, where Satan has clearly set his sights on the church, on the family, and on believers.

We live in a culture that is obsessed with sex—before marriage, outside of marriage, and in perverse forms. Jesus said that in the last days, there would be wicked times as in the days of Noah and of Lot (see Luke 17:27–29). These both were times in human history uniquely characterized by sexual perversion.

Adultery has spread throughout society, and we see its effects in broken marriages and displaced children. I have seen varying statistics on infidelity and I doubt anyone can really know the accurate numbers. Suffice it to say they're too large. And if you think this is a problem unique to men, think again.

So significant is the sin of adultery that it made the top ten: the Ten Commandments. "You shall not commit adultery," God says (Exod. 20:14). Then God expanded on it: "You shall not covet your neighbor's wife" (v. 17). He said this for our own protection.

You might be thinking, *I really don't need to hear this. I would never fall into sin. My spouse and I have an ideal marriage.* I trust that as a Christian, you are committed to staying far away from adultery—or even thinking about it. But it's one of those sins that sneaks up on you, despite what you think, if you do not have your guard up. Satan likes to come in stealth mode, stealing in when he finds a hole in your defenses. I want to give you some ammunition this week, so that you will be able to keep your guard up to battle any temptations that could lead you astray.

I remember listening to an interview with a man who had written some Christian books on the family. This man had boasted to his friends, "If I ever fall into sin, I guarantee it will not be adultery. Anything but. I love my wife so much that it would never happen to me." Do you know what happened? You guessed it. He fell into the sin of adultery. He concluded by saying, "An unguarded strength is a double weakness."

Whenever we say things like, "I would never fall into that sin," we are on thin ice. After all, 1 Corinthians 10:12 tells us, "If you think you are standing firm, be careful that you don't fall!" Don't think that somehow you are above something—that you would never fall into a certain sin. You are capable of doing the worst things. So am I.

You have heard the story of Samson and Delilah. Samson deluded himself into thinking: *I am the mighty Samson. I can kill a thousand Philistines with the jawbone of a donkey. What is one little woman going to do to me?* But the devil was sly. He knew he could never bring Samson down on the battlefield, so he brought him down in the bedroom. It was a sneak attack through Delilah, whose name, ironically, means "delicate." She began to break down Samson's resolve until he finally confessed to her the secret of his supernatural strength (see Judg. 16:16–21). If only he could have realized he was falling into a trap.

Infidelity—whether emotional or physical—destroys marriages. Even if you've never been tempted in this direction, do not be cavalier about it. As Proverbs 4:23 says, "Above all else, guard your heart, for it is the wellspring of life."

PONDER

Even though inappropriate thoughts inevitably pop up into every person's mind, we do not have to entertain them. Such thoughts are not sin, but dwelling on such thoughts is essentially rehearsing for rebellion, and acting on such thoughts is sin. We can't keep from being tempted, but we can avoid rehearsing, and we can certainly refuse to sin. No temptation becomes sin without our permission.

—SHANNON ETHRIDGE[37]

PROBE

- In what ways do you personally struggle with the messages our immoral culture sends? How do you keep yourself protected?
- Why is it so dangerous to be confident of your ability to avoid a certain sin?

PRAY

Pray that the Lord would help you build a fortress around your family to protect you from the immorality of today's culture.

32

STEP BY STEP

In the spring, at the time when kings go off to war, . . . David remained in Jerusalem.

2 SAMUEL 11:1

*U*sually the steps that lead to sexual immorality, including adultery, are numerous. It happens over a period of time.

We see this in the life of one man who committed adultery and paid the price for it in the years to come. His name was David. Most of us know the story of David and Bathsheba. It all happened when the kings were going out to battle, but David was taking some time off (see 2 Sam. 11). In the small missteps that lead to sin, this was David's first. He was not on the battlefield where he was supposed to be. Instead, he was home, and it seems he may have even been bored.

He certainly was idle. He was out strolling on his balcony when he looked down and saw a beautiful woman named Bathsheba bathing herself. Now, he couldn't have avoided that first look—but the second one is probably what got him into trouble.

He then began to devise a plan in which he could have Bathsheba. Misusing his authority as king, he commanded Bathsheba to be brought up to his chambers. He had sexual relations with her, and Bathsheba became pregnant. But instead of confessing his sin to God, he tried to cover up what he had done. So he sent word that Bathsheba's husband, Uriah, who was serving David in his army, was to be brought back to be with his wife.

Uriah was brought back, but David hadn't counted on the fact that Bathsheba's husband was such a valiant and loyal subject that he could not bear to have the pleasure of being with his wife when his fellow soldiers were out risking their lives. So he slept outside that night.

David should have stopped right there. It was as though God was putting an obstacle in his path, trying to warn him. But David persisted. He got Uriah drunk, then sent him to be with his wife. Again, Uriah would not have relations with his wife.

So David ordered his commander to have Uriah sent to the front lines, where he was killed in the heat of battle. Then, without wasting much time, David took Bathsheba into his home and married her.

David may have thought he pulled it off, but it doesn't work that way. The Bible says, "He who conceals his sins does not prosper" (Prov. 28:13). For twelve months, David lived separate from the harmony and fellowship with God that he loved so much. He wrote in the Psalms about the pain of alienation from God that occurs when there is unconfessed sin, and his words still ring true to any who have ever been in a similar position:

> When I kept silent,
>   my bones wasted away
>   through my groaning all day long.
> For day and night
>   your hand was heavy upon me;
> my strength was sapped
>   as in the heat of summer. (Psalm 32:3–4)

His sin weighed heavily on his heart; he may have kept the secret, but it was killing him.

Eventually David was confronted by a prophet of God, and the king finally confessed his sin. The Lord told him he was forgiven, yet there were ramifications for this series of sinful actions. It started when the son conceived by David's adultery died seven days after being born. It continued in ongoing strife down through generations of David's family.

If you are engaged in unconfessed sin right now, sexual in nature or not, in action or even in the realm of the imagination, then you know the agony that David is talking about. You know the destruction that sin can bring, and the weight of it as it sits on your soul. You know the lack of peace that consumes you. If you choose to continue in your sin, then you are choosing self-destruction. And know this—your sin will catch up with you. Scripture reminds us, "Be sure that your sin will find you out" (Num. 32:23). No one ever gets away with sin.

But if, instead, you bring your unconfessed sins to God and invest in your marriage, you are choosing life.

PONDER

Like quicksand, temptation always urges, always pulls, always sucks us deeper into its depths. The moment we step into it, we feel a steady, downward tug on our ankles. Initially, we can free ourselves by resisting the pull and stepping back onto solid ground. But the longer we stay in, the deeper we sink, until we are in over our heads.

—LINDA DILLOW AND LORRAINE PINTUS[38]

PROBE

- Why is it so destructive to cover up your sin? Do you think it's possible to get away with it?
- What are some examples in your life of a series of small steps leading to big mistakes? What could you have done differently?

PRAY

Ask God to reveal to you any sins you have been reluctant to confess. Begin confessing each one and genuinely repenting.

33

FORGIVENESS IS KEY

*The punishment inflicted on him by the majority
is sufficient for him. Now instead, you ought to
forgive and comfort him, so that he will not be
overwhelmed by excessive sorrow. I urge you,
therefore, to reaffirm your love for him.*

2 Corinthians 2:6–8

Sexual sin can devastate a marriage—but the wonderful grace of God can repair the damage inflicted even by adultery. As a pastor, I've seen and heard stories of couples who have survived and come through the devastation caused by adultery. I've seen God use these trials in marriage to bring couples closer together and closer to Himself. I've even seen couples destroyed by infidelity to the point of divorce and witnessed God's miraculous hand in teaching forgiveness and bringing restoration.

Cheryl and Jeff Scruggs, who lead an organization called Hope Matters Marriage Ministries, were married for several years before their marriage was wrecked by adultery that ultimately led to a painful divorce. Even though they were apart, God was working in both Jeff and Cheryl's hearts. Cheryl writes:

After we had been divorced for seven years, God restored our shattered marriage. Jeff and I remarried on a beautiful Sunday in October of 1999. The day was surreal and overwhelmingly filled with the Spirit of God. We struggled to contain ourselves in seeing this miracle come to fruition. We will never stop praising God for the glorious gift He gave in redeeming our brokenness. I stood trembling, trying not to fall to my knees, and looked at my beautiful husband with humble gratefulness. I could not believe we had spent seven years apart. But God knew exactly what He was doing.

Cheryl's story bears wonderful testimony to the biblical promises that God can indeed give beauty for ashes, joy instead of mourning, and praise in place of despair (see Isa. 61:3). Yes, with the help of the Lord, a marriage can survive even the desolation of adultery.

I am not excusing this sin. God doesn't, and neither should we. Yet there is a difference between a man or a woman who has fallen into adultery but has confessed and repented and wants to make the marriage work, and an unrepentant individual who persists in infidelity without remorse. God forgives anyone who confesses and repents of his or her sin, no matter how hideous, and He calls us to do the same.

God not only forgives our sins, but in His marvelous wisdom and grace, He can take the mess we have made and still be glorified through it. That is not to say you were right in doing what you did, but at the same time people can see God extend mercy, grace, and a second chance, giving hope to you and others. But having said that, let me remind you that there are often lifelong consequences for our sins. Though forgiven, David reaped what he sowed many times over. His own children followed his example of immorality and even murder.

When a young man in Corinth who had committed adultery with his stepmother repented, the apostle Paul told the church to "forgive and comfort him, so that he will not be overwhelmed by excessive sorrow" (2 Cor. 2:7). That should always be our attitude toward the truly repentant. It's a different ball game with the habitual sinner who has no intention of changing, even when caught. God Himself will deal with that individual (see Heb.13:4).

Bottom line? Even in cases of marital unfaithfulness, divorce is not commanded. Jesus says simply that it is permitted (see Matt. 19:8–9). If adultery has taken place, every effort should be made to restore the marriage. Remember, unfaithfulness is not only grounds for divorce—it is also grounds for forgiveness. Psalm 103 says,

> He does not treat us as our sins deserve
> > or repay us according to our iniquities.
> For as high as the heavens are above the earth,
> > so great is his love for those who fear him;
> as far as the east is from the west,
> > so far has he removed our transgressions from us. (vv. 10–12)

If at all possible, we ought to aim for reconciliation, because God loves to take something as colorless as the ashes and create stunning glory out of it—beyond what we can imagine.

PONDER

Forgiveness . . . is the single most significant tool we have for meeting and for healing the troubles which marriage shall surely breed between us. What those troubles will be, we do not know. But that they will be, we may be assured. And nothing—neither our love, our effective communication with each other, our talents, our money, nor all the good will in the world—no, nothing can make right again the wrongs as can forgiveness.

—WALTER WANGERIN JR.[39]

PROBE

- What transgressions of your spouse have you held on to and avoided forgiving? What might you do to begin extending forgiveness for those?
- What do you find the most difficult about forgiving those who have hurt you?

PRAY

Ask God for the grace and strength not to condemn others but to forgive as He does.

34

SIX REASONS TO NOT BE UNFAITHFUL

I made a covenant with my eyes not to look
lustfully at a girl.

JOB 31:1

$\mathcal{Y}$ou may feel as if you don't need this chapter, but please read it anyway. If you are ever in the least bit tempted to consider unfaithfulness, even if it's just in your heart, you will need this ammunition to help you fight the battle. In that perilous hour, you might even want to turn back to this page.

Reason #1: You Damage Your Spouse

If you are involved sexually with someone besides your spouse, whether or not you feel it "means anything," it violates the sacred bond you have with your spouse. Paul wrote, "Do you not know that he who unites himself with a prostitute is one with her in body? For it is said, 'The two will become one flesh'" (1 Cor. 6:16).

That is why infidelity violates the very fiber of the marriage (see Matt. 5:32). It takes the one sacred act that only husband and wife are supposed to share and degrades it. That's not to say you can't experience forgiveness or healing. But recovery is a difficult and painful process.

Reason #2: You Damage Yourself

To get into the place where you're willing to commit adultery, you have to harden your heart. You have to distance yourself from God and forfeit whatever fellowship you've built with Him. That hurts you spiritually. You also have to harden your heart against your spouse and your children. You have to turn a blind eye to the way in which you're hurting them. You have to tell yourself you don't care, when in fact, you probably do. And you put yourself at risk physically, with AIDS and other diseases running rampant. So you see, infidelity can damage you in every way: spiritually, emotionally, and physically.

Reason #3: You Damage Your Children

A man dramatically undermines his position as spiritual leader in the home if he commits adultery. His children's trust in him— not to mention the trust of his wife—has been eroded. Children may, in turn, even repeat the same sin. How can you teach your children to be sexually pure when you are not?

As I already stated, God forgave David of his sins, but David's children still paid the price. Two sins that David himself had committed, sexual immorality and murder, were also committed by his children. Your children will look at your example.

Reason #4: You Damage the Church

Scripture teaches that when one member suffers, the whole body suffers (see 1 Cor. 12:26). As believers, we are interconnected. The victories and defeats of individuals affect the body as a whole. That is why Paul told the believers in Corinth who had a sexually immoral man in their midst initially to remove him from their fellowship. He told them, "A little yeast works through the whole batch of dough" (1 Cor. 5:6). Once the man had repented, he was readmitted into the fellowship of the church.

Reason #5: You Damage Your Witness

As the prophet Nathan said to David after he had sinned, "By doing this you have made the enemies of the LORD show utter contempt" (2 Sam. 12:14). It is one more thing for unbelievers to hang their doubts on.

Reason #6: You Sin Against the Lord

This should be the primary reason we avoid sin. But I think many Christians today lack the fear of God. You love God so much that you don't want to do something that would bring shame to His name.

When Joseph was tempted by Potiphar's wife, he responded, "How then can I do such a wicked thing and sin against God?" (Gen. 39:9). Joseph didn't say, "What if your husband walks in? He will kill me!" or "It could ruin my career!" He didn't want to sin against the Lord. That is the highest motive of all.

PONDER

Fidelity is not simply abstention from sex with other persons. It is a positive regard for the dignity of the partner and an attitude of thanks for the partner's self-offering. My beloved requires it of me, and I require it of my beloved.

—THOMAS E. BREIDENTHAL[40]

PROBE

- What other reasons can you think of for not being unfaithful?
- What should you do if you find yourself in a situation in which you're tempted to be unfaithful emotionally or physically?

PRAY

Pray that God will give you the strength and the wisdom to flee from temptation long before you need this list.

35

THREE WAYS TO AVOID ADULTERY

Flee from sexual immorality.
1 CORINTHIANS 6:18

So what steps can we take to prevent the devastating sin of sexual immorality? What can we do to build a wall of protection around our lives and around our marriages?

1. Walk with God

It's simple but true. If a husband or wife is truly walking with God, he or she will have the power to stand strong against temptation. It was David's failure to do this that made him vulnerable to the temptations he faced.

Walking with God means proactively developing your relationship with Him. It means seeking Him relentlessly, through Bible study, prayer, and fellowship with other believers. It means that you apply yourself each and every day to move in the direction God wants you to go. It means surrounding yourself with godly influences. And it means being honest with Him at all times about what's in your heart. If you sense yourself starting to go astray, talk with Him about it immediately.

If there is something in your life, whether it's a relationship or something you are doing, that is leading you toward temptation, then you need to stop. Ask God for the strength, and let Him help you through the hard parts. It could be an e-mail relationship, phone calls, frequently traveling on business, or watching suggestive movies and television programs. Whatever it is, if you sense you are going in the wrong direction, you need to nip it in the bud—in the realm of your mind. Stop it now, before it is too late.

You should be willing to give up whatever is necessary to keep from falling into sin. Whatever steps you have to take to prevent you from falling morally or spiritually, take them, even if they are drastic, like finding a new job or relocating. The Bible says, "Live by the Spirit, and you will not gratify the desires of the sinful nature" (Gal. 5:16). The best defense is a good offense. So walk with God.

2. Walk with Your Spouse

Enjoy a close and intimate friendship and romance with your wife or husband. At the very foundation of a marriage, and what is missing in many marriages, is that a husband and wife should be companions and friends.

You also need to keep the romance alive in your marriage. Cultivate it. If the romance is dying, then throw some more logs on the fire. Do what you can to rekindle it again. Do all you can to sexually fulfill each other.

The Bible tells you, "Drink water from your own cistern, running water from your own well" (Prov. 5:15). Find fulfillment in your marriage relationship as husband and wife, as God has created you and has blessed that union.

3. Don't Flirt with Danger

Avoid, at all costs, any friendship that could cause you to fall. If you are in that kind of relationship with someone right now, if you're flirting, then it's time to throw on the brakes. "Oh, it's innocent," you might say. Listen: you never know what it can lead to. Avoid it at all costs—avoid even the appearance of evil.

Count the cost. Remember some of the warnings we've been looking at. These, along with an intense love for God and your spouse, can see you through the rough waters of sexual temptation.

Temptation will be around as long as we live. But we don't have to fall into it if we take the steps God has given us. And if you have fallen into it, stop. Repent. Don't continue in it. Thank God there is forgiveness, and learn from your mistakes.

God won't give us more than we can handle. He won't let us be tempted above our capacity to resist. It is not a sin to be tempted. Jesus was tempted, after all. But it is a sin to give in to temptation. You have a choice in the matter. Choose harmony and love over infidelity and destruction.

PONDER

But the feeling of love for someone other than your spouse is downright dangerous. Everything in you will encourage you to spend more time with this person who makes you feel so good, even if it is a threat to your spouse. . . . If you ever find yourself infatuated with someone other than your spouse, don't walk away, RUN!

— Dr. Willard F. Harley Jr. and Dr. Jennifer Harley Chalmers[41]

PROBE

- Of the three ways given to avoid falling into immorality, which do you need to work on the most? How can you get started?
- Think of more ways to avoid falling into sin, and make a list. Then pray over it, asking God to help you put these new hedges into place.

PRAY

Ask God to reveal to you any activities or relationships you're presently engaged in that could be harmful to you and your spouse. Do what you need to do to remove them from your life.

A CHRIST-CENTERED MARRIAGE

We have discussed many aspects of marriage by now, from the ways we love and stay committed, to the ways we communicate and keep ourselves pure. This week gets to the heart of the Christian vow, as we delve into what it means to have a Christ-centered marriage. As you read through this week's selections, pray for God to be with you, enlightening you and helping you to understand what He wants you to learn here.

36

HONORING GOD

So whether you eat or drink or whatever you do,
do it all for the glory of God.

1 Corinthians 10:31

Sometimes Cathe and I will be out somewhere and we'll notice an older couple—in their eighties or so—walking along holding hands. Have you seen that? Doesn't it make you long for that kind of enduring, happy marriage?

For some reason, it often seems like an impossibly optimistic dream. Marriage is difficult and the way out is just too easy. We may be committed to staying married "as long as we both shall live" but sadly, we are not always as dedicated to making our marriages wonderful, happy, safe havens. Life teaches us that sometimes, we have to "settle" for less than the ideal.

I don't think God desires for us to settle for anything less than His best in our marriages. When I speak with couples whose marriages have lasted happily for fifty years or more, they always seem to have a few things in common. They verbally say "I love you" often. They work to forgive each other for the daily small hurts, and the occasional large ones as well. They recognize that we are all fallen people, and that their spouses are never going to be perfect. They work to understand each other's differences so that they can appreciate each other's strengths.

But perhaps the most important characteristic in these marriages is their unity of purpose: they put Christ first, and everything else is secondary. They recognize that marriage is one of the ways in which God forms and refines us, and their goal is to glorify God through their marriage. Therefore they meet every obstacle with the question: "How can I honor God in this situation?"

What does it look like to honor God in all things? When that is your highest goal, it's easier for you to navigate disagreements. Since you each desire to honor God, you always have a foundation of commonality from which to start. Your opinions may diverge from there, but by continually coming back to the shared objective of honoring God, you can negotiate in a manner that is loving, honest, and fair.

Honoring God in all things also means staying away, to the best of your ability, from temptation, which is obviously a great advantage to your marriage. If your reverence for God compels you to avoid keeping company with corrupt people or being influenced by our depraved society, you will never "blame" your spouse for keeping you from these evils. You will always know why you are being so careful about your behavior. It is for God, not man.

It is important to honor God in your thought life too. As the apostle Paul puts it, "We take captive every thought to make it obedient to Christ" (2 Cor. 10:5). This means we are submitted to Christ even in our minds. When we find ourselves daydreaming about an attractive person we've met or thinking vengeful thoughts about someone who's angered us, we must give those thoughts up to God and recognize that we are sowing seeds that could turn into deeds. We need to allow Him control in our thoughts, in this way honoring both Him and our marriage.

Your mate is a gift from God. As such, work on loving your husband or wife as the unique person he or she is. You cannot make your mate into what you want him or her to be. But you can help your spouse be all that God wants him or her to be. The longer you walk with your mate, the closer you will come to finding the pleasure of living every day together.

Would you like to have a long-lasting and fulfilling marriage?

Then make sure you are honoring God in all things. Spend time aggressively developing friendship and romance in your marriage. The more time you spend cultivating these things, the less interest you will have in seeking them elsewhere. The many long and successful marriages I've seen prove that following Christ's design for intimacy between a husband and a wife produces a security, love, and fulfillment that cannot be found anywhere else.

PONDER

God is still in the business of creating marriages. He desires to be the foundation stone of each union. Most marriages are based on nothing; it is not surprising that many collapse. But it is never too late with God. At any point, if we turn over our lives and our marriages to Him, He will become the foundation, the builder, and the rebuilder, if that is necessary, of that home. Even the broken pieces of our lives can be mended and repaired if we let God be God in every area of our human relationships.

—JACK MAYHALL[42]

PROBE

- What is the difference between wanting your spouse to change and wanting to help your spouse be all that God wants him or her to be?
- List some ways you can do better at honoring God in all things, especially in your marriage.

PRAY

Ask God to reveal any ways in which you are not honoring Him, and pray for wisdom and the ability to mature in these areas.

37

A STRONG FOUNDATION

*Therefore everyone who hears these words of mine
and puts them into practice is like a wise man who
built his house on the rock. The rain came down,
the streams rose, and the winds blew and beat
against that house; yet it did not fall, because it
had its foundation on the rock.*

MATTHEW 7:24–25

The foundation on which you build your marriage will determine its staying power. So what's the best foundation? The Bible leaves no doubt: "Unless the Lord builds the house," says Psalm 127:1, "its builders labor in vain." The proper foundation is essential.

So may I ask—is your marriage built on the Rock, or is it heading for the rocks? Is your union built upon Jesus Christ and His unchanging Word, or on the shifting sands of human opinion and emotion? Your answer makes all the difference.

If your marriage is built on the Rock, then you will carefully listen to what Jesus says through the Scriptures. You will hear His words and gladly commit yourself to obey whatever He tells you. In so doing, you declare with King David,

> The LORD is my rock, my fortress,
>   and my deliverer;
> my God is my rock, in whom I take refuge,

my shield and the horn of my salvation.
He is my stronghold, my refuge and my savior. (2 Samuel 22:2–3)

Nothing—not even catastrophe—can ultimately shake you.

On the other hand, if your marriage is not built on Christ, you will probably ignore His instructions. You may continue to attend church services and Bible studies, but you'll feel no desire or obligation to actually do what Jesus says. And if that's the case, you will be like Jeshurun, who "abandoned the God who made him and rejected the Rock his Savior" (Deut. 32:15).

The foundation you've chosen for your marriage will reveal itself clearly when the storms hit. Jesus said that the rain will descend in torrents, the floodwaters will mount, and the winds will roar. Into every marriage a little rain must fall. Sometimes it's a light drizzle; at other times it's El Niño! But every marriage will be tested.

Perhaps you're wondering whether your marriage really is built on the foundation of Jesus Christ. Or perhaps you already know that it's not. Please don't despair. Anytime you choose, you can turn your marriage over to God and allow Him to become the Rock. You can begin honoring God through all things, including your marriage, and He will welcome you. Even if you are married to a nonbeliever or an inactive or marginal Christian, you can see to it that *your* life is built on the Rock, and that *your* part of the marriage is completely dedicated to God.

One couple speaks about this very thing:

We attended church sometimes but weren't believers when we married, and our marriage definitely wasn't built on Christ. Well, when trials finally hit, they nearly did us in. We had nothing to fall back on and were headed straight for divorce court. Luckily there were quite a few Christians praying for us, and we are sure that's what made the difference.

Out of nowhere, each of us suddenly felt convicted to fall to our knees before God and turn it all over to Him. We did this separately, each not even knowing the other was doing it. From that point on, God began to rebuild our relationship. He asked a lot of us, and it was grueling sometimes. But we were committed to total obedience.

Within a few months, we could feel that our marriage had a whole new foundation under it, something solid and not shaky. We hadn't even realized our marriage was so flimsy. But now we knew it was, because we could tell the difference. Today we don't have a perfect marriage—who does?—but we have something we never imagined possible: an unshakable commitment to staying together until death do us part.

Our loving Savior wants us to be ready—and He says that sand just doesn't cut it as a foundation. The only safe way to survive the coming storms is to remain securely anchored to the Rock.

PONDER

God is the Rock who speaks to us, boldly and authoritatively, through the pages of Scripture. The Bible's words are His words. For this reason, we don't have to guess or speculate about the moral issues that confront us in the Bold New World. If we will but take the time to read and listen, the Rock has answers.

—ROBERT LEWIS[43]

PROBE

- Is your marriage built on the Rock? By what criteria do you determine your answer? Would your spouse agree with you?
- What are some steps you could take to strengthen the foundation of your marriage?

PRAY

Pray that Jesus would be the foundation of all you do, think, and decide in marriage.

38

CHOOSE YOUR FRIENDS WISELY

Do not be misled: "Bad company corrupts good character."

1 CORINTHIANS 15:33

$\mathcal{M}$arriage takes a man and a woman and binds them together as one—but a good marriage requires more than just the husband and wife. Those who experience the best marriages, while carefully safeguarding the sanctity of the union, also seek out help and encouragement and counsel from godly friends and family members.

Sometimes I hear a puzzled husband or wife wonder aloud, "Why am I being tempted all the time?" In most cases, it's no mystery. When I ask, "Well, with whom have you been spending time?" I often get answers that boil down to something like, "I just hang out and go to parties with a bunch of people from work." Or they might say, "Well, I travel to conventions quite a bit and spend a lot of time in hotel bars." It's obvious to me why temptation comes calling. When you thoughtlessly participate in the "normal" activities of the world, you set yourself up to fail.

Because the apostle Paul knew this, right after he tells the young Timothy to flee youthful lusts, he advises him to "pursue righteousness, faith, love and peace, along with those who call on the Lord out of a pure heart" (2 Tim. 2:22).

"Get with the godly," Paul advises. "Spend time with those who delight in walking with the Lord."

Why should the apostle give such advice? It's simple. The kind of company you keep plays a big role in the kind of lifestyle you lead. "Do not be misled," Paul writes, "Bad company corrupts good character."

Scripture consistently warns of the dangers of hanging around those who do not love the Lord. Psalm 1:1–2 says,

> Blessed is the man
> who does not walk in the counsel of the wicked
> or stand in the way of sinners
> or sit in the seat of mockers.
> But his delight is in the law of the LORD,
> and on his law he meditates day and night.

Let me go one step further: if you want your marriage to thrive, you need to spend time with those who actively nurture their walks with the Lord—"those who call on the Lord out of a pure heart." Why would you want to follow the counsel of a halfhearted Christian who doesn't think and act biblically, anyway? You need strong Christian friends in the Lord who will "tell it to you straight" and keep you accountable to Jesus Christ, using God's Word as their source.

What if you are in a work environment full of nonbelievers? Your calling is to be salt and light (see Matt. 5:13–16). That means you are to exhibit Christlike qualities so that others can't help but see. But you are not to become really close friends with them if their behavior could lead you astray. Jesus said, "You do not belong to the world, but I have chosen you out of the world" (John 15:19). Yes, you are in this world, full of evil and sin and unbelievers. But you are not *of it*. You are separate.

Even if you generally socialize with fellow Christians, you have to keep your guard up. Unfortunately, I have seen groups of Christians hanging out together and watched as their behavior sometimes veered over into the unacceptable. Don't think you have to follow along just because you're with so-called believers.

So take a good look at the company you keep. Are the men and women who surround you helping you to move forward in your spiritual walk? Or are they pulling you back? If you sincerely want to prevent immorality from banging at your door, you may need to make some changes in the company you keep. Spend time with the godly, and you'll soon begin to discover the "eternal pleasures" to be found only at the right hand of God (see Ps. 16:11).

It's a good idea to find other spiritually strong couples you can spend time with. They can be a tremendous example to you and, as your marriage gets stronger, in time you can do the same for another couple.

PONDER

Do not protect yourself by a fence, but rather by your friends.

—Czech Proverb[44]

PROBE

- What activities are you participating in, and what people are you associating with, that could lead you into temptation? What can you do about it?
- What is the most difficult part of choosing our friends wisely?

PRAY

Ask that God would reveal to you any changes you need to make in your activities or social relationships.

39

IT DOESN'T JUST HAPPEN

One thing I do: Forgetting what is behind and
straining toward what is ahead, I press on toward
the goal to win the prize for which God has called
me heavenward in Christ Jesus.

PHILIPPIANS 3:13–14

You sometimes hear it said that a couple has "a marriage made in heaven." But what's the flip side of that—a marriage made in hell? It's as if some people believe that good marriages just sort of tumble out of the sky and that bad ones ooze up from below. The truth, of course, lies elsewhere.

Good marriages do not just happen. They are not the surprise result of good fortune or the fortuitous combination of pleasant genes. Good marriages take work—hard work, long work, persistent and creative work. For good reason, happy marriages sometimes get compared to successful athletic teams.

The best teams do not simply happen. Occasionally, the managers of some professional teams appear to think that all they need to do is to collect a boatload of talent, and the championship is theirs. But almost never do such teams end up winning the big games. When playoff time comes and they have to face teams that have worked hard to learn how to play together as a unit, they lose. Talented groups of individuals can never consistently outperform hardworking, well-meshed teams.

And the amazing thing is, the harder these well-oiled teams work to function as a unit, the more effortless their play appears to be to observers. Players anticipate the moves of teammates and end up scoring almost before their opponents recognize the threat. They're just fun to watch, almost as if the team were . . . made in heaven?

But of course, it wasn't. To get to this level of excellence, team members have to put in long hours of practice together, working through problems, smoothing out conflicts, polishing roles, learning how best to encourage one another, trying new approaches.

It's really no different in marriage. Certainly God loves to bless and enable husbands and wives to build their marriages into loving units of championship caliber, but no good marriage is simply "made in heaven." Behind the success and the confetti and the celebration lies a whole lot of determined work.

Happy couples put to work in their marriages the same mind-set that drove the apostle Paul in his faith: "One thing I do: Forgetting what is behind and straining toward what is ahead, I press on toward the goal to win the prize for which God has called me heavenward in Christ Jesus."

Sometimes couples come to me with problems, and after we talk, they agree that it's going to be hard work, and they are willing to do whatever it takes to improve their marriages. A few weeks or a few months later I'll ask, "How's it going?"

"Well, I guess it's going fine," they might say. "But I just didn't realize it was going to be so hard!" I always have to smile because that's the way most of us are. We talk a good talk, but walking the walk is a whole different story!

You need to acknowledge to each other, husband and wife, that sometimes marriage is hard. Then, when you are having a difficult week, or a particularly sticky disagreement, you can look at each other and say, "Well, this is what they meant when they said it would be hard!" That in itself can give you the strength to persevere. You knew it was sometimes going to be hard, and you said you'd do it anyway. So do it.

Be sure of one thing: a happy and lasting marriage is no accident. If you see a good marriage, realize it is the result of considerable applied effort. I guarantee you that this couple isn't problem-free and always in agreement 100 percent of the time. They put in the effort and stick with it through thick and thin. It may not be a marriage made in heaven, but it's definitely a marriage celebrated there.

PONDER

I visited in an office one time where there was a sign: "In ten years what will you wish you had done today? DO IT NOW!" That's good advice for the Christian home builder. We need to form a mental image now of what we want for our home and children ten years from now.

—HOWARD HENDRICKS[45]

PROBE

- In what ways do you find the "work" of marriage to be different than what you expected?
- How are you and your spouse doing at teamwork? What could be improved?

PRAY

Ask God to be the captain of your team and to keep you motivated for all the hard work that still lies ahead.

40

WHAT IT LOOKS LIKE

But as for me and my household, we will serve the
LORD.

JOSHUA 24:15

So let's get practical. What exactly does a Christ-centered marriage look like? I have identified some basic characteristics that we all can strive for in our marriages.

In a Christ-centered marriage, husband and wife both accept Jesus Christ as their Lord and Savior. They believe in the teachings of Scripture and are building their lives on the example and principles of Jesus. Their mutual goal is to glorify God through their lives and their marriage. Both partners are committed to preserving the marriage despite any ups and downs. They believe and understand God's proclamation that "the two will become one flesh" and consider themselves joined by God and therefore not easily separated. Even when the going gets rough, neither partner looks at divorce as an option but instead looks for ways to restore and revitalize their partnership.

This couple enjoys worshiping together. Being part of a strong church is a vital aspect of their walk with God. They intentionally make time to study and discuss Scripture together, and they make prayer a central aspect of their lives. They pray together and for one another.

Husband and wife display mutual love and respect. They exhibit unconditional love for each other in all its facets: sacrificial love, ac-

tive love, and servant love. The marriage is founded on a commitment to fidelity in heart, mind, and body. Both partners understand
the importance of faithfulness to God's commands and to each other,
being careful not to compromise their marital vows by becoming
overly or inappropriately involved with anyone or anything outside
the marriage.

The relationship between husband and wife is characterized by
the fruit of the Spirit. Love, joy, and peace are evident in their coun-
tenances. Their marriage exhibits patience, kindness, and goodness.
They are recognized by their faithfulness, their gentleness, and their
self-control.

In a Christ-centered marriage, Christ is also at the center of par-
enting. Children are raised according to biblical principles and taught
about Christ. They are part of a church along with their parents, and
they learn Scripture from an early age.

The couple has a good understanding of submission and authority. They are mutually submitted to Christ and to each other. They follow God's plan for the husband to be head of the wife, and Christ the
head of the husband. Neither the husband nor the wife manipulates
or uses the concept of submission to his or her advantage. The marriage exemplifies the concept of selflessness. Both spouses do their
best to put the other's needs ahead of their own, following God's lead
in all things. Both exhibit a giving spirit, striving to give as much of
themselves as they can, first to God and then to each other.

Husbands and wives accept their differences, both as individuals and as men and women. They have an appreciation for how God
created us male and female and value the uniqueness in that design.
They do not strive to be the same in all ways but rather to complement each other.

Couples in a Christ-centered marriage will enjoy a satisfying intimate life together, as they share their bodies and very lives in the way
Christ intended. They attempt to keep a spark of romance going as
much as possible, so that their love stays bright and alive. And finally,
husbands and wives practice forgiveness continually. They accept

each other's fallen state as humans but glory in each other's beauty as creatures of God.

Of course, this is a portrait of an ideal couple—one that doesn't exist! Let it be an inspiration to you as you continue developing your Christ-centered marriage.

PONDER

The Christian's ultimate call is not the call to develop a good marriage; the Christian's call is to be a disciple of Jesus Christ. . . . If we follow biblical guidelines for marriage, this relationship can enhance our growth as disciples of Christ. It can provide for us an opportunity to practice such principles as servanthood and unconditional love. But as Christians, we must remember that marriage is not an end in itself. Individually and as a couple, we are to give ourselves to minister in our community and around the world.

—GARY D. CHAPMAN[46]

PROBE

- How closely are you meeting the characteristics of a Christ-centered marriage outlined here? What could you improve upon?
- List any other characteristics of a Christ-centered marriage you can think of that aren't listed here.

PRAY

Let's pray for Christ to be the center of our marriages.

KINDNESS AND RESPECT

The day-to-day experience of a healthy marriage is made up of small acts of kindness, respect, affection, and care. The big issues will always be there, but your daily attitude can make or break your marriage. Think about how often you give your mate your very best. Then make it a goal to give him or her the best of yourself every single day.

41

CLOTHED WITH KINDNESS

*Therefore, as God's chosen people, holy and dearly
loved, clothe yourselves with compassion, kindness,
humility, gentleness and patience.*

COLOSSIANS 3:12

You might turn to Shakespeare to be entertained, but don't trust the Bard for advice on marriage—at least not the well-worn words from *Taming of the Shrew*: "She shall watch all night / And if she chance to nod I'll rail and brawl / And with the clamour keep her still awake / This is a way to kill a wife with kindness."[47]

Believe me, keeping your wife awake all night with loud noises will not earn you the description of "kind." If you want to see what kindness is all about, look to God. It is His kindness that won us over in the first place. As the apostle Paul reminded us, "God's kindness leads you toward repentance" (Rom. 2:4).

Consider the kindness of Jesus. During a long day of teaching and healing, He still fed the hungry multitudes. In the upper room, though He was keenly aware of His impending death on the cross, He humbly knelt down and washed the dusty feet of His disciples, including those of the man He knew would soon betray Him. When Jesus hung on the cross and bore our sin, He put our needs above His own. He was in pain. He was thirsty. He was in anguish as He bore the sins of the world. But He thought of us. Even after His resurrection, Jesus took the time to fix breakfast for His famished followers.

The Bible contains nearly sixty uses of the word "kindness" and most of the time, it is in reference to God's own kindness. History is full of His unbelievable benevolence toward His rebellious, sinful people. We rarely deserve His compassion, yet He extends it anyway. What a great example to follow. You don't have to wait until your spouse does something special and "earns" it. You can practice being kind as a regular, daily part of your marriage. All it takes is thinking before you speak so that your words come out nicely, taking the time to do small favors, and letting your mate know you are thinking of him or her.

Kindness is part of the definition of love in 1 Corinthians 13. So as we love our mates, we should naturally exhibit kindness. It is also part of the fruit of the Spirit in Galatians 5:22–23. The only way to manifest the fruit of the Spirit is to have our lives joined with Christ. The Spirit produces the fruit in us—we cannot manufacture it ourselves. So one of the ways we can increase our kindness is to make sure we are constantly loving and seeking the Lord.

Your kindness has the power to change the entire character of your marriage. It determines the atmosphere of your home and how your spouse relates to you. It determines how your children view you, and of course, how people outside your family see you. It is one small virtue with giant rewards.

Make it your goal to express your love in practical acts of kindness. As corny as it may sound, thoughtful gifts such as flowers or a gourmet meal still go a long way. Why not surprise your wife with an unexpected little gift? If you come home with a present and say, "I want to tell you that I love you and I care about you," your act of kindness will do more than you could ever imagine to nurture your love for each other. Even something as simple as a kiss and a few loving words can make a profound difference, because kindness is an active ingredient in *agape* love.

So, when did you last kiss your mate and say, "I love you"? Love is kind. Tell your spouse that you love him or her today.

PONDER

One of the most difficult things to give away is kindness; it usually comes back to you.

—Author Unknown

PROBE

- Can you think of a time someone was kind to you even though you really didn't do anything to deserve it? How did it make you feel?
- Think of at least ten ways you could be kind to your spouse this week.

PRAY

Thank the Lord for His unequaled kindness and ask Him to produce it in you.

42

THE SIMPLE THINGS

*Husbands, in the same way be considerate as you
live with your wives, and treat them with respect.*
1 PETER 3:7

$\mathcal{I}$ rarely leave for work without kissing Cathe good-bye. It's a small thing, but it says something important. It tells my wife that I love her, and it reminds me as I walk out the door that I have an incredible friend and partner to come home to. I enjoy heading out for the day feeling connected to Cathe, knowing that nothing can separate us.

It is often in doing the simple things that husbands and wives express love to each other. A brief expression of affection, a kind word— these can make all the difference in your day, and when you add up years full of days, they have the power to change your life! Yet how often do we see husbands and wives being more polite to complete strangers than to each other? They engage in more conversation with their coworkers than with their spouses. They'll do a good deed for a neighbor and forget the needs of their families. Sadly, couples that have fallen into this pattern have lost sight of their priorities.

Part of the problem, I believe, is a certain blessing in marriage that also can become a curse: being comfortable with each other. Of course, we can and should be able to let our guard down in our homes. Who would want to walk around at home wearing formal clothes all the time? But sometimes, in our ease, we can go a little too far. We start wearing the same old, dirty T-shirt day after day or neglect basic grooming.

The same thing can happen in the way husbands and wives communicate. They are abrupt. They interrupt. They don't listen to each other. Although we want to be loved and accepted by our spouses, we need to be careful that we don't become so comfortable that we forget our manners and forget to be respectful.

The definitive passage on love, 1 Corinthians 13, tells us that "love suffers long" (v. 4 NKJV). This means that you allow your mate to change in God's timing. Also, as we saw on Day 12, it says that love does not envy. It does not boast. It is not puffed up. It does not behave rudely. This means that you treat each other with respect. Remember, the Bible refers to the church as the "bride of Christ." This means the way we interact as husbands and wives should be an example of Christ's relationship to the church and our relationship to Him. There is and should be a good deal of reverence—awe, even—in our relationship with Christ. Don't you think that could be in our marriages too?

In the Christian life, we start off with certain basics that keep our walks with God strong and vibrant. When we begin to neglect those basics, our spiritual lives begin to slow down. This can happen in marriage as well. The exciting love that set your marriage into motion is kind of like an engine starting. Then the motor needs to run. You need to maintain the discipline of doing the simple things, even when you don't feel like it. This is not something you do once and always remember; rather, it is a constant process. It will take diligence and awareness and fine-tuning along the way. I once heard a quote: "Love doesn't just sit there, like a stone; it has to be made, like bread, remade all the time, made new." [48]

We would do well to post that in our kitchens! When God sent the Israelites manna in the desert, they had to collect it fresh every day. No living off yesterday's manna! It's the same with the love in our marriages. We've got to seek to make it fresh every day.

The secrets of a successful marriage are not all that numerous.

Often the biggest factors are the smallest things: kindness, respect, and affection. Paying diligent attention to these everyday virtues is not difficult and can bless and strengthen our marriages.

PONDER

The root of most marital problems is sin, and the root of all sin is selfishness. Submission to Christ and to one another is the only way to overcome selfishness, for when we submit, the Holy Spirit can fill us and enable us to love one another in a sacrificial, sanctifying, satisfying way—the way Christ loves the church.

—WARREN WIERSBE[49]

PROBE

- Why do you think it is so important to pay attention to the simple things in marriage like kissing your spouse in the morning?
- In what ways have you become "too comfortable" around your mate? Can you think of any changes you might make?

PRAY

Pray that the Lord would be in control of your marriage, and His presence would remind and inspire you to do the simple things each day.

43

DWELL WITH UNDERSTANDING

Husbands, likewise, dwell with them with
understanding, giving honor to the wife, as to
the weaker vessel, and as being heirs together of
the grace of life, that your prayers may not be
hindered.

1 Peter 3:7 (nkjv)

There's a lot to be said for knowing someone extremely well—especially if that someone is your wife.

The term translated "dwell" in this verse does not mean merely to live with one's wife; it means "to be aligned with" her. In other words, the apostle here tells us that every Christian husband needs to know his wife's strengths, weaknesses, hopes, aspirations, and fears. And such intimate knowledge comes only through frequent conversation, careful listening, and diligent observation. Peter is speaking to husbands, but the advice applies to wives too. You need to know your husband, and you need to honor who he is.

You chose to marry knowing quite a bit about your husband or wife yet also knowing that you would learn more as time passed. The choice brought with it the responsibility to love that person—all of that person. As you grow to understand the depth of your mate's heart and mind, choose to embrace all of who he or she is.

One woman told writer Nathaniel Branden:

My husband has always been my best audience. Whether it's something I did at work that day, or a clever remark I made at a party, or the way I dress, or a meal I've prepared—he seems to notice everything. He lets me see his pride and delight. I feel like I'm standing in the most marvelous spotlight. I only hope I'm as good at expressing my appreciation of him, because I'll tell you something: being loved is the second-best thing in the world; loving someone is the best.[50]

This woman anticipated Peter's next instruction to Christian husbands. Not only are we to gain a deep understanding of our wives, but we are to use that knowledge to honor them. Do you think this woman felt honored? Of course she did; that's why she felt as if she stood "in the most marvelous spotlight." And did you notice her natural response? She aimed to do for her husband what he did for her, match his appreciation for her with an equal appreciation of her own. And so begins the most delightful competition in the world.

Husband, what does your wife need right now? Do you know the problems or struggles she faces? What are her dreams? Just how well do you know your wife? And how are you using your knowledge to honor her?

Wife, what could your husband use right now? What's weighing on his mind? What is he worrying about? Does he allow himself to dream for the future?

We honor our mates by *knowing* and *caring* about who they are. But husband, it's not enough to just know and care—you also have to show it. That's how you honor her. You have to speak words and take actions based on knowing who she is. A surprising number of husbands find themselves in a counselor's office or on a divorce attorney's couch because they failed to honor their wives. They didn't even know what they were neglecting at the time, but their wives felt it every single day.

If you're not honoring your spouse, Peter has a word of warning for you. He tells husbands that failure to honor our wives by dwelling with them in an understanding way puts up a big roadblock to answered prayer. So if you have been praying lately and have noticed there does not seem to be much of a response, ask yourself: *Am I honoring my wife the way God has told me to?*

PONDER

For a marriage relationship to flourish, there must be intimacy. It takes an enormous amount of courage to say to your spouse, "This is me. I'm not proud of it—in fact, I'm a little embarrassed by it—but this is who I am."

—BILL HYBELS[51]

PROBE

- Why do you think Peter gave his exhortation to husbands and not to wives?
- Why does God place such a high premium on husbands honoring their wives?

PRAY

Ask God to keep you tuned in to your spouse's needs, desires, dreams, and moods.

44

WITHOUT WORDS

Wives, in the same way be submissive to your husbands so that, if any of them do not believe the word, they may be won over without words by the behavior of their wives.

1 PETER 3:1

$\mathscr{I}$'ve mentioned that women tend to be more verbal than men. Although there are exceptions to the rule, women generally speak more than men do. According to Gary Smalley, women speak twice as many words a day as men do. By dinnertime a man is talked out, while his wife still has a whole day's worth of words in her. I've seen this play out in the way men and women answer the phone. When a man answers the phone, he reaches for a pencil. When a woman answers the phone, she reaches for a chair!

There is a limit, however, to what words can accomplish. The apostle Peter said that unbelieving husbands are more easily won to the Lord by the way their Christian wives live than by what they say. A woman named Denise made that discovery with her own husband:

My husband and I were not Christians, but when our daughters were young, we found a wonderful church and pastor who cared enough to bring us into the fold and teach us what a relationship with Jesus really was. Eventually our family joined the church and my husband and I both accepted Christ as our Savior.

From that day on, I was on fire for the Lord! I attended Bible study, read Scripture every day, and developed an active prayer life. I looked at our baptism as the start of a whole new journey. My husband, however, saw it differently—his view was more like: "I'm saved—cool. What's next?" He wasn't interested in developing a relationship with Christ, reading the Bible, or praying.

At first I would encourage him to pay attention to his spiritual walk, but he just felt nagged. Then my pastor told me that I should not say anything to my husband about it. He said my own behavior and the obvious joy I was experiencing in the Lord would have to be my silent testimony to my husband.

This went on for about five years. Then suddenly a huge crisis hit our lives. My husband had always been so self-sufficient, but this time he felt powerless. He thought about all those years that I'd been relying on Jesus for my strength. For the first time in his life, this strong man dropped to his knees and admitted his powerlessness before God. He apologized for being lukewarm (or even cold) in his faith and asked God to come into his life—for real this time. Our lives have never been the same since.

Because this woman hung onto God's Word and did what it told her to do, she can testify that Peter's words were right. Her husband finally decided to follow Christ because of five years of seeing her walk that path. Today she is full of joy and gratitude to be walking the faith journey alongside her husband, instead of alone.

If God can use your actions to make such a big change in someone's life, He certainly can use your actions in daily life to bless your spouse in smaller, but no less important, ways. If you find yourself in situations where you and your spouse are arguing frequently, or you are habitually nagging about something, try stopping altogether. Concentrate on fewer words and more love. If nothing else, the fact that your tirades have ended will certainly give him or her pause; and hopefully as you show kindness and embody loving behavior, your spouse will be motivated to make the change you were working so hard to encourage.

If your spouse is a nonbeliever or a marginal one, your best strategy is to model the Christian life and pray for him or her. Although there will be times when it's appropriate for you to talk about your walk with God, you don't need to overwhelm your partner with the gospel message everyday. Just live it out.

I believe it was Saint Francis of Assisi who said, "Preach the gospel, and when necessary, use words."

Often the best way to communicate is without words. Why not give it a try?

PONDER

The ancient philosopher Zeno once said, "We have two ears and one mouth, therefore we should listen twice as much as we speak." A wife who follows this advice will not only be obeying God's command to be quick to hear but will be coming one step closer to really loving her man.

—LINDA DILLOW[52]

PROBE

- Think of one thing in your marriage that seems to cause repeated strife. What would happen if you stopped talking about it and instead tried to just be loving and kind?
- Wives, what is scary about being told not to talk so much? Husbands, how would you react if you noticed your wife was talking less?

PRAY

Pray that you would each have the grace and perception to talk and listen just the right amount for your marriage.

45

IRRESISTIBLE BEAUTY

> *Wives, . . . do not let your adornment be merely*
> *outward—arranging the hair, wearing gold, or*
> *putting on fine apparel—rather let it be the hidden*
> *person of the heart, with the incorruptible beauty*
> *of a gentle and quiet spirit, which is very precious*
> *in the sight of God.*
>
> 1 PETER 3:1, 3–4 (NKJV)

Although it's never wise to emphasize outward appearance at the expense of the inner life, neither should wives neglect the outside while nurturing the inside.

The word the apostle Peter used here for "adornment" comes from the Greek term *kosmos*, from which we get our English word *cosmetic*. Peter warned women to avoid focusing on physical appearance to the detriment of the soul.

It is interesting to look at old engravings from the Roman era. The women had amazing hairdos. They piled their tresses high into towering coiffures interwoven with golden braids. They wore gold rings on every finger and attached gold all over their clothes. Peter paints a picture here of a woman who flaunts her wealth; the phrase "putting on fine apparel" means the frequent changing of attire. He warns against a woman's deliberately dressing in such a way as to be noticed in the church assembly, thus prompting men to gaze on her body instead of worshiping God. Peter is saying, "Concentrate on the inner woman."

At the same time, women should not completely neglect their outward appearance. This passage warns against focusing on the outward; in other words, strike a balance. The Bible certainly does not forbid a woman to present herself in an attractive way. Looking sloppy and unkempt is no virtue—and it can be detrimental to one's marriage.

Anne Graham Lotz, daughter of Billy and Ruth Graham, was interviewed about her parents' love and affection for one another. She told about one visit over a Mother's Day weekend: "Even though mother is almost eighty and has just undergone her fourth hip replacement surgery, when she heard that Daddy was on his way to see her that morning, she got up from her wheelchair, asked me to help her put on a new dress, and fixed up her hair and makeup."[53] Even though Ruth Graham has reached her twilight years, she still puts a high priority on looking her best for her husband.

I recently spent some time with Ruth and Billy in their mountain home in North Carolina. Also present were their son, Franklin, and musician Dennis Agajanian. Ruth asked Dennis to play a song on his guitar. Dennis offered a masterful version of "The Hallelujah Chorus," flat-pick style!

Ruth's face lit up with delight while Billy seemed to be in more of a contemplative mood as the melody filled the room. When Dennis was done, Billy turned to Ruth and said, "That was the song that was played on our first date!"

Apparently, all those years ago Billy had taken Ruth to a concert. It was as if it had happened yesterday for them. The love between them was so real and genuine. It moved me deeply. The inner beauty of a godly woman was apparent that day as I looked at Ruth's face.

Wife, make it easy for your man to keep on staring at you by working with the beauty God gave you. When you take the time to fix yourself up for your husband, you are giving him the unspoken message: *You are special to me. I value you enough to take the time to look attractive to you.*

Keeping yourself attractive is a form of kindness to your husband. You see, God wired your husband to be a visual creature. He enjoys looking at his wife, and when you have taken the time to prepare yourself for him, he derives great pleasure just from beholding your beauty. For a man, this can be a powerful factor in keeping him wanting to come home to you, and only you, every day.

By the way, husbands, this is a two-way street! While your wife may not be as visual as you are, she certainly is sensitive to your cleanliness, your scent, and whether or not you value her enough to look nice for her. Don't let her down by hanging around the house in your torn boxers and 1980s T-shirt. (Unless it's a vintage collectible, in which case you may want to sell it on e-bay.) And don't forget to take a shower! Remember: Soap is your friend.

Women, I'm sure you've noticed the second part of Peter's recommendation, to have a "gentle and quiet spirit," which he classifies as "incorruptible beauty." Many women today struggle with this verse, knowing they are anything but gentle and quiet! But Peter is talking about your heart, not necessarily your demeanor or behavior. You can be an energetic, fun person. But if you cultivate a heart that is kind, gentle, and caring, your husband will surely not be able to resist your beauty!

Husbands and wives, be as attractive as you can be, placing your greatest attention on cultivating the goodness within.

PONDER

The most beautiful of all women seem to have in common some timeless qualities of beauty—grace, wisdom, thoughtfulness, kindness, compassion—and they carry them with a certain sense of confidence. These are the qualities of what I believe to be true beauty. They are accessible to every woman. We need only to put them on and live our lives sheathed in their presence.

—Alda Ellis[54]

PROBE

- Husbands, how does your wife's physical appearance affect you on a daily basis? When do you most like to look at her?
- Why is a woman's "gentle and quiet spirit" precious in the sight of God?

PRAY

Ask God to help you appreciate the inward and outward beauty in your mate.

CONTENTED AND FULFILLED

For this final week, I have chosen Scriptures from the Song of Songs, an intimate story of love and marriage between a man and a woman. Spend this time thinking about the beauty of your marriage and the blessing it really is. Celebrate your union, and thank God for your spouse, that one special person He has given you to cherish, enjoy, and love forever.

46

MORE PLEASING THAN WINE

How delightful is your love, my sister, my bride!
How much more pleasing is your love than wine,
and the fragrance of your perfume than any spice!
SONG OF SONGS 4:10

Song of Songs, written by King Solomon, is a beautiful story portraying the delightful thrill of falling in love and making a lasting commitment. This lyrical poetry captures the passion, the ecstasy, and the depth of an epic romance. It is here that we see the pleasure and contentment that God intended as one of the blessings of marriage.

I declare to you that marriage can be the most fulfilling thing you will know in this life, next to your relationship with God. It can succeed beyond your dreams. It can flourish beyond your expectations. If you and your beloved are following Christ, your marriage can become something unbelievably wonderful in your life.

I challenge you this week to read Song of Songs. It's not very long—it should take you only about fifteen minutes. Read it and be inspired by the loveliness and excitement that can characterize marriage. If you really want to enjoy it, I recommend that you and your spouse take turns reading it aloud to each other. Try different translations as well, such as the NLT and other more contemporary versions.

You see, marriage is more than a lifelong partnership. It's more than a way God helps us grow toward holiness. It's more than a cir-

cumstance for raising children. It's more than a pragmatic business ar-
rangement. It is a setting for the most joy that can be experienced this
side of heaven. It is a God's perfect plan. In Genesis 2:18, God says, "It
is not good for the man to be alone." And so He created a woman to
be the ideal companion for the man. Together they form two halves
of a whole. Together they can find the truest harmony that is avail-
able on earth.

I want to focus these next few days on the fulfillment that can
be found in married life. Yes, marriage is a challenge. Yes, it's hard
sometimes—and *really* hard other times. But at the end of the day, it's
you and your spouse, together with Jesus. In fact, your relationship
with your husband or wife is the one that most closely approximates
Christ's relationship with His church—His relationship with us.

We know there is a difference between temporal happiness and
the deeper experience of joy and contentment that transcends circumstance. Sometimes you may be happy in your marriage, but
whenever you're not, you can still have the unshakable joy of abiding
with another and with Christ throughout your life.

These days, it's too easy to be resigned to an "okay" marriage. If
we're not ecstatic all the time, we tend to eventually accept it. That
seems like a good thing—but not if it causes you to stop lighting the
sparks in your marriage! As Christians, some of us are so committed
to our vow of "until death do us part" that we survive on sheer grit,
rather than on any ongoing attempt to make our marriage wonderful,
life-giving, and fulfilling. Why do we do this? I think it just feels safer
sometimes to avoid getting our hopes up for a happy married life.

But you know what? God never tells us to be safe. In fact, the
Christian life is all about risks. I say, step out right now and declare
that you are going to have a joy-filled marriage. Pray it every day. Do
everything possible to make it happen. Love your spouse selflessly,
actively, and intimately. Seek the Lord first in everything. Chase after
God's best—in your marriage, and in your life.

One of the wealthiest men who has ever lived was married five
times. He is said to have once stated, "I would gladly give all my mil-

lions for just one lasting marital success." He realized that a good marriage is worth more than money or possessions or power. If you're enjoying a happy marriage, you are richer than the wealthiest people on earth. Don't forget to thank God for that!

PONDER

It is God's will that we have true delight with him in our salvation, and in it he wants us to be greatly comforted . . . for we are his bliss, because he endlessly delights in us; and so with his grace shall we delight in him.

—Julian of Norwich[55]

PROBE

- Have you ever been resigned to having an "okay" marriage? Have any of your friends settled for this? How does a person get this way?
- Consider whether you really believe that marriage can be unbelievably wonderful. Why or why not? Write down your thoughts.

PRAY

Ask God to fill you with the hope that your marriage can be all that He intends it to be, and the inspiration to follow His guidance toward making it happen.

47

SWEET CONTENTMENT

Like an apple tree among the trees of the forest
is my lover among the young men.
I delight to sit in his shade,
and his fruit is sweet to my taste.

SONG OF SOLOMON 2:3

There's almost nothing like savoring the sweetness of a crisp green apple, plucked just moments before from a towering tree that now offers cool shade from the late afternoon sun. That's contentment, and that's the lovely picture the Bible provides regarding marriage.

Have you ever thought of your marriage like that—as a source of rich, deep, sweet contentment? You'll find such satisfaction only when you release your unreasonable expectations and delight in what you have.

"As a teenager," wrote Dale Hanson Bourke, "I imagined that I'd marry a man who brought me flowers regularly, called me 'darling,' and never failed to hold the door as I passed through it. I would prepare wonderful, candlelit dinners each night, would wear beautiful robes even on Saturday mornings, and would never, ever nag my husband.

"Fortunately," she continued, "I gave up those dreams long before I had the chance to drive myself or Tom crazy with expectations neither of us could meet. It's not that we've forgotten the place of such nice touches in our marriage; it's just that they aren't the kinds of things that a marriage is built on."[56]

It can be difficult to let go of our fantasies and preconceived notions about marriage. But recognition of reality is the first step in contentment. If we are always comparing our marriages to some nonexistent ideal, of course we will always be dissatisfied. Remember that our culture provides and reinforces these unrealistic, fantasy-like visions of relationships. Overcoming our unrealistic expectations can take some applied effort, because there are forces out there proactively feeding us more of the same all the time.

No one who believes the grass is always greener on the other side of the fence can find contentment. Think about when you were single. You probably said, "I'm so lonely. If only I were married, then I would be happy." But after you were married for a few years, you may have thought, *I remember the good old days when I was single. I could go anywhere and do anything I wanted. Now I have all these responsibilities!* Married people often envy singles, and singles often envy those who are married.

God wants us to be content where we are right now. The apostle Paul wrote, "I have learned to be content whatever the circumstances" (Phil. 4:11). As we've seen, the writer of Hebrews wrote, "Be content with what you have, because God has said, 'Never will I leave you; never will I forsake you'" (13:5). The secret of contentment stems from our awareness of the Lord's constant presence in our lives—and the understanding that His presence is what we need most. Our contentment then spills over into every aspect of our lives.

We want to remain peaceful about all the aspects of our mates or our marriages that are not changeable, and we want to accept them without anxiety. We also need the courage to forge ahead under God's direction, transforming through His power those things He wants us to change. We need His wisdom to know which is which.

I love the words of Psalm 37:4: "Delight yourself in the LORD and he will give you the desires of your heart." The word delight here means "to gladden or take joy in." God doesn't say, "Delight yourself in Me if I give you the spouse of your dreams." Rather, He says simply to delight in Him. If we do that, He promises to give us the desires of our hearts. I believe that as you delight or "gladden" yourself in the Lord Himself, your desires will begin to change, and you will look at your life and your mate with new eyes. And what could provide more contentment than that?

PONDER

It is immature to think that the person I married thirty years ago, when she was eighteen, is the same person now at the age of forty-eight. It is unfair for me to hold her to some youthful expectation I may have had about our relationship. We both have made significant changes—physically, emotionally, spiritually, vocationally. We are different people. Life has developed us, shaped us, molded us . . . hopefully for the better!

—WILLIAM CARMICHAEL[57]

PROBE

- Are there aspects of your marriage or your mate that are not within your power to change, yet you would like to? Begin giving them up to God and asking Him for the ability to accept them.
- What are some of the fantasies about marriage that you need to let go of? How can you start to give them up?

PRAY

Ask the Lord to help you delight yourself in Him, not in your circumstances. Ask Him to make your desires, His. "Not my will, but yours be done."

48

BEST FRIENDS

This is my lover, this is my friend.
SONG OF SONGS 5:16

God ordained that "a man will leave his father and mother and be united to his wife, and they will become one flesh" (Gen. 2:24). It is true that the husband and wife are going to be lovers and will probably be parents. But first and foremost, they are to be friends.

Friendship is central to a good marriage. For some people, this is a no-brainer. My wife, Cathe, and I have always been friends, and it would never occur to me to call anyone else my "best friend." But for others, the idea doesn't come naturally. Many of us relate better to same-sex friends and think of marriage as something separate from friendship. I would like to encourage you to think of marriage not as *different* from friendship, but simply as an *elevated level* of friendship. In fact, the most elevated level possible.

The Bible has plenty to say about friendship. Proverbs 17:17 tells us, "A friend loves at all times." We learn about the importance of one close friend rather than numerous superficial acquaintances in Proverbs 18:24: "A man of many companions may come to ruin, but there is a friend who sticks closer than a brother." Solomon tells us in Ecclesiastes 4:10, "If one falls down, his friend can help him up. But pity the man who falls and has no one to help him up!" Don't all these definitions of friendship apply to your marriage too?

I have noticed that women and men tend to interact with their same-sex friends in different ways. This is no scientific study, just my own observation, but it seems that women need their friends for intimate conversation, while men tend to engage in shared activities. Women do share activities, but their main objective is to talk. Conversely, men certainly do talk to one another, but their main occupation is the shared activity.

Now, don't get me wrong, I think same-sex friendships are healthy and enjoyable. But I also think we can look at the reasons we have friends and see what we can do to nurture that aspect of our relationships with our spouses. Wives, this means making an effort to share some—not all—of your husband's favorite activities.

There was one wife who always said the one thing she'd never do was go rock climbing. Not only was it scary, there just didn't seem to be a point to it, and it certainly didn't look like fun. Wouldn't you know, her husband took up rock climbing. She finally decided to take a women's rock climbing class, just to see if she might be able to join her husband. Did she end up loving it? Well, no. She doesn't love it, but she knows the basics of how to do it. More importantly, she's learned enough so that she can help her husband when he wants to go. Now when they go out rock climbing together, she may or may not scale the cliff. But she gets immense joy being with her husband, and they get to spend leisure time together that otherwise would be time spent apart.

Husbands, I'm not letting you off the hook here! Your wife likes conversation, so if you want to be her friend, make sure you're endeavoring to talk with her. It's not as hard as it seems. Actually, if you can become skilled at asking the right questions, she will most likely do the talking! (However, occasionally your wife will actually ask *you* a question, and then you're stuck: you have to talk.) You might even try (gulp) going shopping with her! It doesn't have to be all that bad.

Sharing leisure activities together and making an honest effort at ongoing conversation are two things that will help make your marriage into the best friendship in your life.

PONDER

What greater thing is there for two human souls than to feel that they are joined for life—to strengthen each other in all labor, to rest on each other in all sorrow, to minister to each other in all pain . . . ?

— George Eliot[58]

PROBE

- What are your own ideas about friendship and marriage? Are you and your spouse best friends? Why or why not?
- What are some things you could do to improve the friendship quotient in your marriage?

PRAY

Ask that God would show you how to love your mate not just as a lover and a partner but as a friend—your best friend.

49

TIME FOR PLAY

Come, my lover, let us go to the countryside,
let us spend the night in the villages.
SONG OF SONGS 7:11

Here is one of the best things about marriage: you have with you the most wonderful lifelong playmate, someone with whom to share laughter, fun, recreation, and relaxation. Indeed, most people who have successful long-term marriages will admit that one of the things that keeps them together is simply taking time to enjoy each other's company.

Tending to your marriage above all else involves effort. Especially in today's hectic world, where all of us are constantly busy, to take time for rest and play we have to first make the effort. We have to set aside time from all our other activities and say, "This is *our* time." And we have to guard that time protectively.

You've no doubt heard the importance of "dating" in your marriage. It's almost a cliché, but every cliché starts with a basis of truth and this is no exception. You've got to spend time alone with your spouse! Whether it's a walk around the block, a night out to dinner, or simply cuddling up on the sofa in front of a movie, time alone together is one of the major building blocks of your marriage. People always talk about "quality time" when it comes to their kids, and it's the same with adults! You need to spend quality time together.

What exactly is quality time? It's time spent focused on each other and enjoying each other's company, preferably *not* while doing anything that *needs* to be done. That's why the date night is so important: it's a respite, a break from the routine. It's time for you to relax and enjoy each other at your best. It's play, and that is not a bad thing with all the pressures and responsibilities husbands and wives face these days.

One of the greatest aspects of play is having a sense of humor, and this is something you can incorporate throughout your family life. Have you ever noticed that when you've had a good laugh at something funny, you feel somehow refreshed or lighter? That's what a sense of humor does for you, and you can use it to keep the atmosphere in your home light and fun and pleasant for everyone.

I always recommend that couples try to get away together on an overnight trip occasionally. This could be one night at a local B&B, or a week or more if you have the time. When you change environments, it makes it easier to relate to your spouse as a friend and a lover rather than as a coparent or business partner. You are removed from the "family business" and can focus simply on each other and having fun. It is one of the most rejuvenating things you can do for your marriage.

Cathe and I enjoy our occasional getaways, and the funny thing is, I'm always surprised at how much fun it is. Even though I'm a vocal advocate of spouses taking time for one another, I'm reminded anew of the incredible ways it enhances our marriage every time we actually get away. The time together brings back the sparks of romance and reminds us of our younger days when we were first in love, and you know what? It makes us fall in love all over again.

Have you noticed that when you spend extended time in the outdoors, in a natural environment like a beach or a forest, it changes your whole outlook on life? You feel more peaceful, and you have a new appreciation of the beauty of God's creation. If you share these experiences with your husband or wife and the two of you experience the pleasures of nature together, it somehow brings you closer together. Getting out into nature—swimming, surfing, hiking, camping, walking, skiing, fishing—is one of the best ways to enjoy leisure time together. The idea of recreation is to re-create—to recharge and be rejuvenated for the hard work of life.

Take the time to enhance your marriage and your faith by setting aside time just for the two of you. It will keep your marriage like new—and it will be fun too!

PONDER

But play . . . hints at a world beyond us. It carries a rumor of eternity. . . . When we play, we nudge the border of forever.

—MARK BUCHANAN[59]

PROBE

- How much time do you and your spouse spend in leisure and fun activities together?
- Plan now for a getaway—a couple hours or a couple weeks, it doesn't matter. Get out your calendar and do it.

PRAY

Pray that the Holy Spirit would inhabit your "play" time, infusing the two of you with loving devotion for each other and for God.

50

ANOTHER LOG ON THE FIRE

I am my beloved's,
And my beloved is mine.
SONG OF SONGS 6:3 (NKJV)

The thought I want to leave you with is that your marriage is not a done deal once the wedding is over. Rather, your marriage is living and growing and changing with the two of you, and it's up to you to keep the fire going strong for the rest of your lives.

We've looked at the types of love in marriage, and the meaning of commitment. We've discussed what it is to leave and to cleave, and we've looked at how we use our words. We've taken on some challenging topics like selflessness, submission, and immorality. And we've explored how to have a Christ-centered marriage and how to find fulfillment in marriage. There really is a lot to keeping a marriage strong, isn't there?

But in the end it all comes down to one thing: God's original plan for marriage, that a man and a woman should *become one*. All the things we've talked about in this book have been different ways to ensure that you are carrying out God's plan for your marriage, that you are doing your part in this mysterious venture of *two becoming one*.

Do what you can, every day, to rekindle the fire of your marriage. Don't let up, and don't let that fire go out.

Imagine that you and your spouse went away to stay in a cozy log cabin, just the two of you. The fire is burning in the fireplace, soft music is playing, and the two of you are stretched out on that bear-skin run just as relaxed as can be. You look into each other's eyes and know for sure that this is the person whom God chose for you. But gradually it starts to get darker in the room, and you notice the fire is dying down. The two of you sit up and watch it fade until pretty soon there is nothing but a single glowing ember.

So you get up, saying, "That's it! The fire's out. It's finished. We'll never have another fire. It was great, but now it's over. We'll just have to go get a new house and a new fireplace." Of course, that sounds ridiculous. What are you supposed to do? Just throw another log on the fire! The sparks will catch and that marriage fire will keep on burning.

That's what I want you to remember. Keep throwing logs on the fire. Keep practicing all the things we've talked about here, so that your marriage stays bright and hot and gives off a glowing light. Keep yourself plugged into the Source—constantly filled with the Spirit. May God bless you and your marriage as you continue on the journey of becoming one.

NOTES

1. A. Skevington Wood, "Ephesians" in *The Expositor's Bible Commentary*, vol. 11, ed. Frank E. Gaebelein (Grand Rapids, MI: Zondervan, 1978), 72.
2. Dr. Larry Crabb, *The Marriage Builder* (Grand Rapids, MI: Zondervan, 1992), 115.
3. Al Janssen, *The Marriage Masterpiece* (Wheaton, IL: Tyndale House, 2001), 69.
4. R. C. Sproul, *The Intimate Marriage* (Wheaton, IL: Tyndale House, 1990), 41.
5. Robert I. Fitzhenry, ed., *The Harper Book of Quotations* 3rd ed. (New York: HarperCollins, 1993), 280.
6. Rosalie Maggio, ed., *The New Beacon Book of Quotations by Women* (Boston: Beacon Press, 1996), 426.
7. Dr. Gary Chapman, *The Marriage You've Always Wanted* (Chicago: Moody Publishers, 2005), 123.
8. Richard A. Swenson, MD, *A Minute of Margin* (Colorado Springs, CO: NavPress, 2003), 80.
9. Max Lucado, *Just Like Jesus* (Nashville, TN: Word Publishing, 1998), 15.
10. ThinkExist.com, "Agnes de Mille Quotes," http://en.ThinkExist.com/quotes/Agnes_De_Mille.
11. Deborah Tannen, PhD, "Sex, Lies and Conversation," *Washington Post*, June 24, 1990, C3.
12. Gary Smalley, *Making Love Last Forever* (Nashville, TN: W Publishing Group, 1997), 141.
13. *Life Application Study Bible*, New International Version (Wheaton, IL: Tyndale House Publishers and Grand Rapids: Mich.: Zondervan, 1991), Table: "God's Unusual Methods," 1787.
14. Phillip C. McGraw, PhD, *Relationship Rescue* (New York: Hyperion, 2000), 261.
15. H. Norman Wright, *How to Speak Your Spouse's Language* (Nashville, Tenn.: Center Street, 2006).
16. Gerald Foley, *Courage to Love When Your Marriage Hurts* (Lovegevity.com). http://www.lovegevity.com/marriage/collectiveguidance/fightingfair.html.
17. USHistory.org, Independence Hall Association in Philadelphia, "The Electric Ben Franklin," http://www.ushistory.org/franklin.
18. The Churchill Centre, Washington, DC, *Winston Churchill Speeches and Quotes*, www.winston-churchill.org.
19. Crabb, *The Marriage Builder,* 115.
20. Tim Stafford, *Finding the Right One* (Portland, OR: Multnomah, 1985), 11.
21. Mark Buchanan, *The Rest of God* (Nashville, TN: W Publishing Group, 2006), 100.
22. Maggio, *Beacon Book,* 572.
23. John Cook, ed., *The Book of Positive Quotations* (Minneapolis, MN: Fairview Press, 1997), 463.
24. Bill Muehlenberg, "The Culture of Self and the Kingdom of God," Matthias Media: Resources for Growing Christians, http://www.matthiasmedia.com.au/briefing/webextra/self.html.
25. Jerry Bridges, *The Pursuit of Holiness* (Colorado Springs, CO: NavPress, 1978), 122.
26. Laura Schlessinger, PhD, *The Proper Care and Feeding of Husbands* (New York: HarperCollins, 2003), 4.

27. Fitzhenry, _Harper Book_, 273.

28. _Ibid._, 276.

29. _Life Application Study Bible_, note on John 15:11, 1913.

30. Al Janssen, _The Marriage Masterpiece_ (Colorado Springs, CO: Focus on the Family Publishing, 2001), 33.

31. Southern Baptist Convention, _Baptist Faith and Message_, section XVIII, "The Family," June 10, 1998. http://www.sbc.net/bfm/bfm2000.asp#xviii.

32. Melanie Chitwood, _What a Husband Needs from His Wife_ (Eugene, OR: Harvest House Publishers, 2006), 77.

33. Floyd McClung Jr., _God's Man in the Family_ (Eugene, OR: Harvest House, 1994), 144.

34. Maggio, _New Beacon Book of Quotations_, 427.

35. Wood, _Expositor's Bible Commentary_, 75.

36. John Piper, _Desiring God_ (Sisters, OR: Multnomah, 2003), 183–84.

37. Shannon Ethridge, _Every Woman's Battle_ (Colorado Springs, CO: Waterbrook, 2003), 75.

38. Linda Dillow and Lorraine Pintus, _Intimate Issues_ (Colorado Springs, CO: Waterbrook, 1999), 94.

39. Walter Wangerin Jr., _As for Me and My House_ (Nashville, TN: Thomas Nelson, 1990), 24.

40. Thomas E. Breidenthal, _Sacred Unions_ (Cambridge, MA: Cowley Publications, 2006), 55.

41. Dr. Willard F. Harley Jr. and Dr. Jennifer Harley Chalmers, _Surviving an Affair_ (Grand Rapids, MI: Fleming H. Revell, 1998), 169, 171.

42. Jack and Carole Mayhall, _Marriage Takes More Than Love_, rev. ed. (Colorado Springs, CO: NavPress, 1996), 17.

43. Robert Lewis with Rich Campbell, _Real Family Values_ (Gresham, OR: Vision House, 1995), 81.

44. The Quotations Page, "Quotations by Subject: Friendship," http://www.quotationspage.com/subjects/friendship.

45. Howard Hendricks, _Heaven Help the Home_ (Wheaton, IL: Victor, 1973), 133.

46. Gary D. Chapman, _Covenant Marriage_ (Nashville, TN.: Broadman & Holman, 2003), 4.

47. William Shakespeare, _The Taming of the Shrew_, Act IV, Scene I (Petruchio).

48. Brainy Quote, "Ursula K. LeGuin Quotes," http://www.brainyquote.com/quotes/authors/u/ursula_k_le_guin.html.

49. Warren Wiersbe, _Be Quoted_ (Grand Rapids, MI.: Baker Books, 2000), 107.

50. Nathaniel Branden, "Advice That Could Save Your Marriage," _Readers Digest_, October 1985, 28.

51. Bill Hybels, _Who You Are When No One's Looking_ (Downer's Grove, IL: InterVarsity Press, 1987), 17.

52. Linda Dillow, _How to Really Love Your Man_ (Nashville, TN: Nelson, 1993), 68–69.

53. Anne Graham Lotz, interview by Larry King, _Larry King Live_, CNN, 18 May 2000.

54. Alda Ellis, _A Gentle Beauty Within_ (Eugene, OR: Harvest House, 1999), 10.

55. Monica Furlong, ed., _The Wisdom of Julian of Norwich_ (Grand Rapids, MI: Eerdmans Publishing, 1996), 29.

56. Dale Hanson Bourke, "The Real Meaning of Romance," _Today's Christian Woman_, September/October 1987, 5.

57. William and Nancie Carmichael, _601 Quotes about Marriage & Family_ (Wheaton, IL: Tyndale House, 1998), 99.

58. Maggio, _New Beacon Book of Quotations_, 572.

59. Buchanan, _Rest of God_, 141.

60. The Book of Common Prayer (New York: Oxford University Press, 1990), 431.